NATIONS OF THE MODERN WORLD

SCOTLAND
Sir Robert Rait, C.B.E., M.A., LL.D., and George S. Pryde, M.A., Ph.D.
Revised by G. S. Pryde.
Reader in Scottish History and Literature, Glasgow

ALGERIA: REBELLION AND REVOLUTION
Joan Gillespie, Ph.D.

AUSTRALIA
J. C. Horsfall
First editor of the Australian Financial Review

EGYPT
Tom Little
Arab News Agency, Beirut

FRANCE
P. E. Charvet
Fellow of Corpus Christi College, and University lecturer in French, Cambridge

MODERN INDIA
Sir Percival Griffiths, C.I.E., I.C.S. (Ret.)
Honorary adviser to India, Pakistan and Burma Association

IRAQ
Brig. S. H. Longrigg
Formerly of the Government of Iraq and the Iraq Petroleum Company and one time Political Officer, Iraq
and
Frank Stoakes
Director of Middle Eastern Studies, St. Antony's College, Oxford

ISRAEL RESURGENT	Norman Bentwich, O.B.E., LL.D. (Hon.) *Formerly Professor of International Relations, Hebrew University of Jerusalem*
ITALY	Gerardo Zampaglione *Italian Diplomatic Corps*
JAPAN	Sir Esler Dening, G.C.M.G., O.B.E. *H.M. Ambassador to Japan, 1952-57*
PORTUGAL	J. B. Trend *Late Fellow Christ's College, and Emeritus Professor of Spanish, Cambridge*
SA'UDI ARABIA	H. St. John Philby, C.I.E., F.R.G.S. *Economic adviser to the late King Abdul-Aziz II, Ib'n Saud*
SOUTH AFRICA	J. H. Hofmeyr, B.A., B.Sc. *Revised by* J. P. Cope *Editor-in-chief of* The Forum
THE SUDAN	Sir Harold MacMichael, K.C.M.G., D.S.O. *One time Civil Secretary to Sudan Government, and Governor-General*
SYRIA AND LEBANON	Nicola A. Ziadeh, B.A. (Hons.), Ph.D. *Associate Professor of Modern History, American University, Beirut*
TURKEY	Geoffrey Lewis, M.A., D.Phil. (Oxon.) *Senior lecturer in Islamic Studies, Oxford*

ALGERIA
REBELLION AND REVOLUTION

ALGERIA
REBELLION AND REVOLUTION

By

JOAN GILLESPIE

FREDERICK A. PRAEGER, PUBLISHERS
NEW YORK

BOOKS THAT MATTER

Published in the United States of America
in 1960 by Frederick A. Praeger, Inc.,
Publishers, 64 University Place,
New York 3, N.Y.

*This book is part of the NATIONS OF THE
MODERN WORLD series*

Library of Congress Catalog Card Number 60-14956

PRINTED IN GREAT BRITAIN

Preface

THIS BOOK is based on my Ph.D. thesis at the Fletcher School of Law and Diplomacy and on visits with both sides in the tragic Algerian conflict. It is hoped that it will both appeal to the citizen interested in international affairs and be of use to scholars in the field. A selected bibliography has been included. The book does not fully analyse French policy in Algeria, which has been done so ably elsewhere, but seeks to present lesser known facts about Algerian nationalism, its historical antecedents and the conduct and aims of the present revolution.

I am indebted to the French Embassy in Washington and to the New York Office of the Algerian Front of National Liberation for documentation of their respective viewpoints, and particularly to the French Army in Algiers and the Algerian Army of National Liberation for making my visits to Algeria so pleasant and valuable. I also wish to thank the numerous friends and associates who helped in the preparation of the manuscript, and who have stimulated my thoughts by many hours of interesting conversations.

JOAN GILLESPIE

WASHINGTON, *1959*

Introduction

I T H A S been said that to every thing there is a season and a time for every purpose. This is the time to tell you something of this book's author and the purposes to which she devoted her life.

Jay Gillespie, my sister, was a complex and paradoxical personality who touched many people in many different ways. This young woman loved deeply and hated fiercely but allowed neither to consume her. She worked hard yet knew how to play; preferred to stand alone yet was not lonely; was utterly disciplined but often seemed to care little; was beautiful but gave little thought to her beauty; had immense courage but seemed not to know fear; had a sense of time running but never considered death; was selfish but rarely for herself; demanded action now but knew how to think of tomorrow.

Her great love was for ideas, particularly the idea of freedom. Similarly, her great hate was for those ideas which denied freedom. She was an idealist *par excellence* and the love of her ideals, although intellectually conditioned, was a profoundly emotional thing. Above all she was a person of action, bound and determined to do what she could in furthering the aims for which she stood.

She had prepared herself well for a career of public service. As an undergraduate she did honour work in political science following which she earned her doctorate in international law and diplomacy. Her contributions included two years as a Foreign Service Officer in the United States Government, a series of magazine and newspaper articles on Africa and finally, this book. Her last trip to Africa, in the summer and autumn of 1959, was to have provided material for a second book on the emerging leaders of sub-Saharan Africa.

She had become enamoured of Africa. In one of her last letters she wrote: 'I am at the Hotel de France in Conakry looking out my window with the breeze blowing off the Atlantic. The view is incredible. A centuries-old cotton tree obscures an island out to sea; a peaceful dhow is passing by the foam-washed rocks. There are windswept palms. It is poetic . . . the kind of place to spend a honeymoon. This morning I have wakened to the sound of song in the streets . . . the government's "investissement humain" – a campaign of voluntary labour to clean up the streets, build roads, remodel villages. The esprit is entirely African – the women sing – colourfully dressed with their babies strapped on their backs; the men dance – then hoe or weed away. It is almost a holiday occasion. If I never write again, it will be because Africa has swallowed me up in her rain, her heat, her intrigue, her charming intriguers. . . .'

Even as these words were written she carried within her a virus which in three weeks would put her into a coma, and in four would end her life. She died on 13 October 1959.

Jay had always believed that the world belongs to the living. But the living, after all, are shaped by the influences of many people. Those who loved and were loved by Jay will always carry her mark. And I am sure she would have been pleased at the thought of her book leaving its mark on someone, somewhere.

KENYON GILLESPIE

NEW YORK,
April 1960

Contents

Preface   vii

PART I

ALGERIA: THE UNIQUE COLONY

1 The *Colon*   3
    The Period of Colonization
    Colon Resistance to Military Rule
    Colon Separatism in 1871
    The *Colons* Obtain Autonomy
    The *Colons'* Heyday
    The *Colons'* Decline
    The Psychology of the *Colon*

2 The Algerian   17
    Algeria Before 1830
    Abd El Kader and Rural Resistance
    Land and Islam
    The Decline of the Algerian Middle Class
    The Urbanites Seek Peaceful Change
    The Young Algerian Party
    Algerian Migration
    Clemenceau's Reforms
    The Blum-Violette Proposal
    The 1944 Ordinance
    The Statute of 1947
    The Psychology of the Algerian

3 1954: The *Colon* and the Algerian   29
       The Population
       Urbanization
       National Origins
       Population Structure
       Distribution of the Labour Force
       Land-ownership and Income Distribution
       Literacy and Illiteracy
       Algeria: Raw Materials and Cheap Labour

PART II

ALGERIAN RESPONSE WITHIN THE FRENCH
SYSTEM

4 The Beginnings of Nationalism   39
       The Bloc of Elected Algerian Muslims
       The North African Star and the Party of the
          Algerian People
       The Algerian Society of Reformist *Ulema*
       The Federation of Elected Muslims

5 The War Period   52
       The Algerian Manifesto
       The Friends of the Manifesto and of Liberty
       The Revolt of 1945

6 Post-War Algerian Political Parties   62
       The Democratic Union of the Algerian Manifesto
       The Algerian Communist Party
       The Movement for the Triumph of Democratic
          Liberties

7 Algeria Under the Statute of 1947   70
       The Crisis of the Moderates
       The Schism of the Extremists

PART III

THE RESORT TO FORCE

8 The Algerian Front of National Liberation and Its
  Army   91
    The Revolutionary Committee for Unity and
      Action
    Leadership of the Rebellion
    Structure of the Front of National Liberation
    Structure of the Army of National Liberation
    Strategy and Tactics

9 The Revolutionary Years   112
    The First Appeal
    Military Problems
    The FLN Absorbs the Parties
    Internationalization Begins Slowly
    The Extension of the Rebellion: 20 August
    The Oran Front and the United Nations
    The State Within the State begins
    The Soummam Conference
    Abortive Negotiations with France
    Terror in the Cities
    The Logistics Problem Solved
    1957: Algeria's Year at the United Nations
    The Autumn Offensive and the Saharan Front
    The 'Melouza Massacre' and the Strange War
    The Frontier Conflict
    Expansion of the CNRA and the CCE
    Negotiations Again Fail
    The Tunisian-Moroccan Good Offices
    The Afro-Asian Solidarity Conference
    The Sakiet Bombing and the US-UK Good Offices
    Accra, Tangier and Mahdia
    The Battle of the Referendum
    The Formation of the Provisional Government

9   The Revolutionary Years   112
      Secret Negotiations Fail
      Another 'Algerian' Election
      Two-thirds Minus One
      Voyage to Peking
      Summary and Conclusions

      Postscript   181

      Selected Bibliography   193

      Index   203

Maps

Nationalist Military Activity
    November 1954   200
    January 1956   200
    August 1957   201
    November 1958   201
Algeria   *facing* 202

PART I

ALGERIA: THE UNIQUE COLONY

Chapter 1

The *Colon*

THE Algerian Revolution stands alone among twentieth-century revolutions in its complexity. It has come at a time when nationalism is sweeping the Afro-Asian world and when many states have already gained independence from the formerly dominant European powers. This trend toward national freedom, so accelerated since World War II by technical advance, the decline of Europe and the spread of the ideas of liberty, came late to Algeria. Great Britain more readily released its colonies, largely shunned military conflicts with them, retained their respect and often their friendship. But France spilled much blood and drained her treasury in losing colonial battles. In many areas, nationalist revolutions meant not only political and military opposition to Western colonialism, but an adoption of some Western ideals, including the famed motto of the French Revolution: Liberty, Equality, Fraternity. Unlike the Europeans, the nationalists in the non-European world had to deal with a clash of cultures. Western-educated or inspired leaders had to select those elements in their own societies they wished to retain or reject – practices which had been unchallenged before the coming of the West. As the *élite* used the native culture to support its conflict with the West, so it also used the ideas of the democratic West to remove the dead weights of a feudal past. This dual process often led to strange mixtures of modern techniques and ancient taboos. By and large, Algeria is another instance of this pattern. It is an anti-colonialist movement using France's own mottoes and the theories of Frenchmen to obtain freedom from

3

Metropolitan France. It is also a part of the cultural and political rise of Islam and the Arab renaissance. It is led by a Western-educated, Western-inspired *élite* and followed by a vast population unschooled in Western ways and concepts. It mixes Marxian revolutionary terminology (learned mostly in Paris) with oaths to Allah. In seeking democracy, it numbers among its enemies not only collaborators with France, but retrograde religionists and feudal landlords.

The Algerian Revolution must also be viewed in the context of a French colonial policy which has emphasized its cultural 'civilizing mission'. This policy in the nineteenth and twentieth centuries sought not only to outdo France's European rivals in the conquest of territory, resources and markets, but also to 'convert the heathen' and spread the gospel of the Sorbonne. French civilization, it was thought, need not be confined to the descendants of the Franks, but could be taught to and shared by all regardless of origin. The greatness of France would be assured not only by the extent of its colonies, but by the loyalty of its colonials. This basic viewpoint was little changed in the twentieth century, although it was to some extent secularized. The Christian religion was no longer an absolute necessity for a good Frenchman.

Besides refusing concessions to the nationalism growing in its colonies, French colonialism became intimately connected with the mystique of France itself. A vigorous and victorious France might have retired from unwilling colonies with the safeguarding of its cultural interests. But the humiliating defeat of 1940 and the subsequent use of North Africa as a retreat and re-invasion point made French physical presence there emotionally and militarily vital to many Frenchmen. General Charles de Gaulle, more than any other single man, contributed to the myth of continued French greatness, fought for an important rôle for France in post-war international councils and evoked the great heritage of the past. The French Union, France's response in 1946 to a nascent but predictable evolution of her Empire, turned out regrettably to be little more than 'old wine' in a new bottle. The French Union Assembly never became a progressive organ of a new era of development, co-operation and peaceful change. Instead, France fought a long war before losing the Indo-Chinese states, and the Tunisian and Moroccan Protectorates won independence in 1956. Algeria, legally distinct from the other possessions as a group of French Departments, was the last to take up arms. A victorious rebellion there would represent for many a final defeat of the often beaten and frustrated French Army, an end to France's status as a great power. On the positive side, a French victory in the Algerian conflict might revitalize the Army and set a positive tone for future relations with France's possessions in West and Equatorial Africa. With the exploitation of the newly-discovered Saharan oil, France might end her distasteful dependence on Middle East sources, particularly resented since the abortive Suez invasion of 1956. The psychology of defeatism in France would wane. New direction would come to internal political life.

The Algerian Revolution has an additional unique factor: the presence in Algeria of a substantial minority which is culturally French and backed by French colonial power. Somewhat similar situations exist today only in Kenya, where the primitive Mau Mau rebellion was suppressed, and in the Union of South Africa, where the local African is still 'on reserve' and has not yet mounted a rebellion against the Government's racial policies. In both cases, the cultural differences between the two communities are so vastly greater from those existing between Europeans and Algerian Muslims in Algeria as to make comparisons invalid. There is no single cause of the Algerian Revolution. But if one may be cited, it is the existence for many years side by side of these two disparate ethnic, political and economic groups. The dominance of the Europeans made the Algerian Muslims a kind of 'minority-majority' in their own territory – a numerical majority enjoying only the rights of an oppressed minority. With time, an explosion seemed inevitable.

THE PERIOD OF COLONIZATION

European settlers or *colons* entered Algeria soon after French conquest in 1830. The decision to invade was made by King

Charles X primarily to save his tottering régime. By such an expedition he hoped to divert internal political discontent and also permit France to pose as a Western crusader against the pirates of North Africa. A financial dispute between the French Government and the ruling Dey of Algiers provided the immediate cause. In 1827, the enraged Dey struck French Consul Duval with his fly-whisk during an audience – or so the notorious Consul alleged. To avenge the insult, the French fleet blockaded Algiers without success for over two years. The French expedition landed at Sidi Ferruch in June 1830, and the Dey capitulated on 5 July. Algerian resistance led by the young Emir Abd El Kader continued, however, for some seventeen years.

While the colonialists and the anti-colonialists in France debated whether the Government of King Louis Philippe, successor to Charles X, should keep its newly acquired possession, the first *colons* went to Algeria. They came from various parts of the Mediterranean world, and for diverse patriotic, adventurous or economic reasons. In the period of 'free' colonization from 1830 to 1840, French soldiers settled with government encouragement; wealthy investors bought estates; Spanish peasants migrated to Western Algeria; and Italian, Maltese and Corsican peasants and fishermen found their way to Eastern Algeria. In 1834, King Louis Philippe reluctantly made Algeria a French possession, and in 1840 it was decided to conquer all of the territory.

The appointment of General Bugeaud as Governor-General in 1840 opened a period of 'official' colonization. The advocates of this type of colonization wished to see Algeria a colony of small French peasant settlements and believed that such immigrants would not go to Algeria without official assistance. Free land was made available, along with the Army's help in clearing roads, planning settlements and erecting buildings. From 1848 to 1852, official colonization increased rapidly. The revolutionary years in Europe and the 1852 *coup d'état* of Napoleon III in France brought political exiles to Algeria, although only a few had an interest in rural settlement.

Napoleon III favoured free colonization; and the *colons* themselves were beginning to dislike the State control which official colonization implied. A third stimulus came from the increasing liberalization of trade between France and Algeria which began at mid-century. Under Napoleon III, large land concessions were made to investors, in the hope that they would carry out some of the aims of French policy by establishing villages on their estates. These large concessions, along with similar ones made later, still constitute the basis for many *colon* fortunes in Algeria. They did not, however, greatly contribute to small French settlements there.

Colon Resistance to Military Rule

As the *colons* increased in number, they sought more important rôles in both their local government and the formulation of French policy. In July 1834, General Drouet d'Erlon became the first Governor of 'French possessions in the North of Africa'. The selection of a General as Algeria's first Governor-General, holding both civil and military powers, underscores the military nature of France's rule. While the *colons* agreed with the Generals who favoured complete occupation of Algeria and official military and civilian colonization, they disliked the extensive and arbitrary powers exercised by the French Army of Africa on the local scene.

In 1848 the *colons* were successful in curbing the power of the military. By a decree of 4 March of that year, the pacified, civil portions of Algeria were made 'an integral part of France'. The Governor-General retained only military powers, while finance, justice, education and related matters were put under their respective ministries in Paris. Separate civil and military territories were established, including three Departments, each sending a deputy to the French Parliament. This structure was, however, short-lived, and the Napoleon III 1852 Constitution excluded Algeria from legislative representation. In 1858, Napoleon temporarily ended the continuing struggle between the civilians and the military by creating a Ministry for Algeria and the Colonies, thus re-establishing a civil régime.

The Governor-General remained a military man, however, and the primacy of the military administration did not end until 1870. Even thereafter, military men occupied the post of Governor-General for some years. By a decree in October 1870, Algeria – now roughly the area north of the Sahara Desert – was officially proclaimed three French Departments under the Ministry of the Interior. By 1875, each Department was entitled to send one deputy and one senator to France; by 1881, each had two deputies. In March 1871 a civil Governor-General, directly responsible to the Ministry of the Interior, was named.

COLON SEPARATISM IN 1871

The decade prior to 1870 saw an increasing hostility develop between conservative *colons* and Napoleon III. The *colons* objected to Napoleon's concept of Algeria as his 'Arab Kingdom' in which the local Algerians, as well as the European immigrants, were entitled to the protection of their French monarch. The *colons* also criticized the Catholic Church for its efforts to educate and uplift the local Algerian population. At the fall of Napoleon's Second Empire in the Franco-Prussian War, the *colons* in Algeria attacked and insulted the French military and formed Committees of Defence and Public Safety. In November the ageing Governor-General, General Esterhazy, was beaten and put out of office. In this first major show of *colon* separatism, overtures were made to Garibaldi of Italy and the British Queen. But the new French provisional government soon reestablished its control over Algiers.

The last three decades of the nineteenth century saw increasing colonization of Algeria, both private and official, as well as certain changes in the character of the European population. Algeria also underwent considerable agricultural and commercial development. The Franco-Prussian War gave Alsace-Lorraine to Germany, and many families, wishing to remain French, migrated to Algeria. In 1870, Algerian Jews were made French citizens. At the same time, a revolt of the Kabyles and other tribes led to the confiscation of large tracts of land,

providing new land for incoming migrants. In 1878, the blight
on French vineyards brought a number of wine-growers to
Algeria.

Despite official colonization efforts, French citizens did not
greatly outnumber other Europeans in Algeria. In 1839, of
25 000 settlers, only 11 000 were of French origin. In 1847, of
about 110 000 settlers, 48 000 were French; 32 000 were
of Spanish origin; and 8–9000 each were Italian, Maltese, and
Germans or Swiss. In 1860, Frenchmen numbered 120 000 of
200 000 settlers. In 1871, there were 130 000 Frenchmen and
115 000 other Europeans in Algeria. In 1876, the numbers were
about equal. In 1889, the naturalization of persons born in
Algeria of foreign parents was made automatic. For the first
time, then, Frenchmen in Algeria clearly outnumbered
Europeans of other origins.

Frenchmen continued their migration to Algeria for many
years, while other foreign migration dropped off considerably
after 1895. Immigration was cut off during World War I, but
the 1936 census still showed about 12% of the European population had been born in France itself. After World War I, fewer
peasants went to Algeria, while skilled workers, tradesmen,
businessmen and government workers increased. The progressive mechanization of agriculture after 1920 may be
responsible in part for this trend, as well as the declining supply
of good land. Most of the official colonization following World
War I was made possible by reorganization of lands already
in use. Local Algerian Muslims became entitled to receive
lands in 1947, thus ending official colonization as such.

The Colons Obtain Autonomy

During the last decade of the nineteenth century, the *colons*
used their new-found economic strength to exert political
pressure on France. Before 1870, they had sought the intervention of Paris to assure their rights as Frenchmen in the face
of arbitrary military rule. After 1870, they received that
civilian control; and Paris followed a policy called 'assimilation', treating Algeria as nearly as possible like other French

Departments. However, disagreement soon arose between the *colons* and the Paris Government of the Third Republic over economic and other expenditures within Algeria and over the future rôle of Algeria's Muslims. Many *colons* believed the Muslims should be exterminated and would eventually disappear, while liberals in France considered the Algerians should be trained as cheap labour. The wealthy *colons*, who favoured autonomy, were by this time able to exert influence in Paris. In 1894, Premier Jules Ferry recognized the failure of the assimilation policy and created a Superior Council of Algeria with sixty members, of whom only seventeen were Muslims. In 1896, France loosened her ties with Algeria; and by 1900 Algeria received control over her own finances. Under an 1898 law, the Algerian Financial Delegations were created, composed of twenty-four Muslims and forty-eight *colons*. These Delegations, which voted on the Algerian budget, have been called the *colons*' 'Bastille, which dominated the country from 1898 to 1945 . . .'.[1] Both the *colons* and the Muslims on the Financial Delegations represented large landowning interests. Up to 1914, the *colons* showed little concern for Muslim welfare, and unrest among the Algerians was attributed to outside influences.

During World War I, many *colons* fought under the French flag. Some became discouraged and never returned to their Algerian homes. After the war, the *colons* opposed the granting of reforms to Algerian Muslims who had also fought for France. The campaign waged against Premier Clemenceau's proposals included threats of separatism similar to those made in 1871, protests, petitions and pressure from the *colon*-financed North African lobby. But, Clemenceau refused to yield and the reforms were enacted.

THE COLONS' HEYDAY

The first four decades of the twentieth century have been called the heyday of the Algerian *colons*. Even so, the first murmurs of Algerian Muslim nationalism were heard; and Algeria suffered several economic setbacks. A severe wine crisis in the early '30s led French growers to demand cuts in imports from Algeria. Again only the threat of separatism and of boycott of French products prevented tariff discrimination against Algerian wine, although the planting of new vines was thereafter subject to limitation.

In 1936, the Popular Front Government of Socialist Premier Léon Blum sought to satisfy the demands of moderate Algerians by permitting a certain number of educated Muslims to become French citizens without abandoning their personal status under Muslim laws on marriage, divorce, inheritance and the like. *Colon* resistance to this Blum-Violette proposal (named after the Premier and one of his Ministers) was so strong and so effective that it was never discussed in Parliament.

THE COLONS' DECLINE

World War II disrupted the daily lives and prosperity of many Algerian *colons*. Again many left their homes to fight for France. Those who remained were largely sympathetic with the authoritarian and anti-Semitic policies of the Vichy Government of Pétain and Laval. The Atlantic Charter and the North Allied landing of 1942 aroused the hopes of Algerian Muslims, but increased the fears and suspicions of the *colons*. These feelings appeared justified with the brief Muslim revolt of May 1945. Despite the abortive uprising, the *colons* again had to fight post-war French-proposed reforms for Algerian Muslims. *Colon* efforts were not as successful as in 1936; and in late 1947 a Statute for Algeria was voted by the French Parliament. For the first time, Frenchmen and Muslims in Algeria received equal legislative representation in an Algerian Assembly. Although the *colons* were unable to defeat the Statute in Paris, the legislation was never fully implemented and elections were widely rigged. The *colons* remained in political control of Algeria during the years between the Statute and the outbreak of rebellion in 1954. The rebellion brought them face to face with a new threat to their economic and political dominance – this time not from French liberals whose actions they could control or subvert, but from the

Muslim minority-majority whose victory would mean their complete defeat.

THE PSYCHOLOGY OF THE COLON

Much has been said about the psychological make-up of the *colon*: he is a racist, an individualist, a bitter-ender, a paternalist; he is many things. Of course, the views of Senator Henri Borgeaud, Algeria's King of the Vine – so named for his vast grape-growing estates – and Georges Blachette, the Alfa King who owns many acres of alfa grass used in fine paper making, differ widely from those of the clerk in the Government General in Algiers or the Spanish-origin olive tree grower. None the less, the *colons* appear to hold a number of common attitudes: the wealthy *colon* has somehow imposed his views on the 'little *colon*' who does not share his interests. And the rebellion has further submerged any internal rifts. Many of the settlers came to Algeria out of patriotic motives; and many survived under conditions of poor health and military insecurity. But by the latter part of the nineteenth century, economic motives predominated, and life was no longer the hazardous adventure of the early days. In 1892, French Premier Jules Ferry, himself a colonialist, commented about the *colon*:

> We have scrutinized him closely . . . and have found him extremely limited. It is surely not a mental capacity which permits the *colon* to become the arbiter, even to a limited extent, of the fate of the natives. He is not wanting in virtues; he has all those of the hard worker and patriot; but he does not possess what one might call the virtue of the conqueror, that equity of spirit and of heart, and that feeling for the right of the weak which is not in the least incompatible with firmness of command. It is hard to make the European *colon* understand that other rights exist besides his own, in an Arab country, and that the native is not a race to be enslaved and indentured at his whim. The *colons* announce that the conquered race is incapable of improvement or education, without ever having made

any effort to raise it from its moral and intellectual poverty. . . . Undoubtedly there is no intention of destroying the natives nor of pushing them back, but there is no interest in their complaints nor in their number, which seems to grow with the poverty.[2]

In his book, *Dans la Bataille de la Méditerranée*, French General Catroux, who has long experience in French colonial administration notes that the *colons* are

. . . above all beings under the sway much more of the commandments of instinct than of the deduction of reason and the influence of the ideal. They have remained, through atavism, that which their fathers were at the beginning of their settlement in Africa, pioneers, men of action and isolated men, carrying out none the less with an admirable energy and good success enterprises of personal character and interest. They form, as a result, a collection of individuals much more than a delimited collectivity organized on a body of principles and traditions. They come together only for the defence of their interests. But these interests, which are the interests of a class, do not always coincide with those of France. There is lacking in these men, otherwise of good will and whose persevering effort has transformed arid Africa into fertile land, a sentiment of spiritual values, a less materialistic and egotistical conception of relations among men and therefore of the native problem. They lack the generous ferment of a disinterested culture and the taste for ideas, the absence of which is accentuated with the years that pass and with the increase in prosperity.[3]

Jean Daniel, a liberal French Algerian, wrote in the French newspaper *L'Express* on 4 June 1955:

These French of Algeria have more than one point in common with the Southerners (*esclavagistes*) of the United States: courage, dynamism, narrowness of views, the sincere conviction that they are born to be masters as others are born to be slaves, (that to change these natural inequalities is to introduce disorder), and affection for servants if they wish to remain servants. . . .

Louis Lavie, a fourth generation *colon*, sheds interesting light on the psychology of the *colons* from a differing point of view. He notes with fervour: 'Countries belong to the men who have known how to form them, to develop their population, to give them institutions, and to assure their intellectual and material life.' With regard to the rebellion, Lavie comments: 'Each Frenchman must understand . . . that the struggle which his brothers of Algeria are carrying on has no other aims but those of defence of the common Fatherland and the safeguarding of Christian civilization, in the largest sense of the word, on the soil of Africa.' Lavie concludes that the ideal of Christian civilization was the *raison d'être* of France and made her greatness. The end of the ideal, in grave danger in Algeria, would risk the collapse of France itself.[4]

These observations serve to underline certain common attitudes created by the colonial system itself. The *colon*, like man as a whole, is the child of his environment – an environment numerically hostile to him and to his culture as long as the Algerian Muslim is not permitted to share it. Such an environment takes from the *colon* the 'luxury' of democratic solutions in his ever-present conflict with the Algerians. For such solutions would undermine the very basis of the *status quo* from which the *colon* so richly profits. Assimilation of the minority-majority is not a real alternative in the mind of the *colon*, for it would both change the nature of the dominant French culture and provide unwelcome competition. This in turn would remove the attraction which first brought many of the *colons* to Algeria. This political and economic necessity is often translated by the *colon* into a sense of racialist superiority, thus making impossible a challenge to his privileged status.

The attitude of the *colons* toward France and continental Frenchmen is mixed. Because they are far from France, the *colons* sometimes see few of her faults and tend to make her their ideal motherland. But when France's Government does not support *colon* against Muslim, when *colon* pressures fail, disappointment is the greater and the reaction the more violent. All the same, France's military protection has become necessary for the *colon's* very existence in Algeria since 1954. And the *colon* wishes to associate his position in Algeria with French greatness, and his culture with French culture in a conflict which has so many cultural overtones.

The 'alliance' of 13 May 1958 between the French Army and the *colons* to force France to 'keep Algeria French' was not an unnatural one. *Colon* fear that a weak French Government would negotiate a political settlement with the rebels was running high. But the *colon* could not threaten secession, although there was talk of it, because it would deprive him of the vital protection of the Army. Now the enemy of the embattled *colon* was not a liberal France proposing to uplift the downtrodden Algerian Muslim, but the Algerian himself demanding a new way of life with gun in hand. For a moment, the *colon* with Army support was able to forestall negotiation, to impose his will on Paris. But the Army demanded a victory for its own and a revival of French glory, not continued *colon* predominance. And the Army took control.

The events since the 13 May 'alliance' have brought out the worst in the *colon* psychological make-up: his racism, his defiance of authority, his selfish outlook. He has adopted the Army's formula for an Algerian solution—integration—out of no love for the Algerian Muslims. This was the very assimilation which his stronger ancestors rejected in 1900. On the eve of the elections, hot-headed young *colons* were calling for a twenty-year dictatorship in France – an extreme solution, but one which few *colons* would oppose. The 'decadent' French across the water would then have to share the burden that even a token integration of Algerian Muslims would impose. The young generation realized that integration, while there was a weak government in France, would only submerge the *colons* in a Muslim sea.

The vast majority of the present *colons* were born in Algeria and know little of life in France. Their desire to retain their special privileges is mixed with their natural affection for a beautiful country. But the rebellion which they have done so much to prolong has also made them think of the future. The lines have gradually been drawn, although little is said about it, between those who will leave and those who will stay should Muslim Algeria win its rebellion. Some wealthy *colons* already possess properties in France to which they can 'retreat'. Poorer *colons* may remain and become Algerian citizens or ask for French aid to migrate elsewhere if conditions became unacceptable.

REFERENCES

[1] Julien, *L'Afrique du Nord en Marche*, p. 43.
[2] Cited in Julien, *L'Afrique du Nord en Marche*, cited by Stevens, *North African Powder Keg*, p. 20.
[3] Cited in Julien, *L'Afrique du Nord en Marche*, p. 43.
[4] Lavie, *Le Drame Algerien*, pp. 27, 97.

Chapter 2

The Algerian

ALGERIA BEFORE 1830

THE ORIGINAL inhabitants of the Maghreb – the Arab 'West' consisting of present-day Morocco, Algeria and Tunisia – were Berber tribes, whose ancient historical origins are still obscure. To the strong loyalties of the tribe, the Berber added individualism, democratic participation in inter-tribal affairs and fierce opposition to foreign invaders. Over the centuries, many conquerors came to the Maghreb, but few established durable empires, and few exercised a significant cultural influence. In the religious sphere, the Berbers continued to practise their animistic beliefs, while often adopting religious heresies to oppose their Christian, Jewish or Islamic overlords. Throughout the history of the Maghreb there seems to have been a conflict between the sedentary farmer and the pastoral nomadic peoples—a strife which was often exploited by the invaders from other lands.

Prior to modern times, the most significant invasions of the Maghreb were those of the Phoenicians, the Romans, the Vandals, the Byzantines, the Arabs and the Turks. Of these, the Arab invasions of the seventh and the eleventh centuries left the most important cultural imprints on the people. During the Roman era, agricultural areas expanded at the expense of the nomads, and the Maghreb still boasts of well-preserved ruins of Roman amphitheatres, aqueducts and columns. The breakdown of Roman rule, however, and the Vandal and Byzantine invasions led to an expansion of pastoral lands. The first Arab invaders came from village areas in the Middle East and therefore tended to favour the farmers in the Maghreb. The conversion to Islam of the Berber tribes, many of which were either Jewish or Christian at this time, began in the early eighth century. To oppose their Arab conquerors who became despotic, the Berbers accepted the Kharijite heresy of Islam. Extensive Islamization and Arabization did not occur until the devastating Hilalian invasion of the tenth and eleventh centuries brought nomadic Arabs from Arabia to North Africa. The Hilalians gave their Bedouin Arab tongue to the North African Berbers, and extended the pastoral areas at the expense of farms and villages, which they mercilessly pillaged.

The first Arab invasion of the Maghreb coincided with the high tide of Arab power in the Mediterranean world. With Berber assistance, the invading Arabs went on to conquer Spain and reached Poitiers in France in 732. Their defeat there by Frankish King Charles Martel was followed by their retreat, due in large part to Berber resistance to Arab policies in the Maghreb. The subsequent centuries were marked by political instability and occasional flowering of cultural life in North African cities. Trade in gold, slaves, salt and other exotic commodities was carried on with Negro kingdoms south of the Sahara. This peaceful commerce along with conquests by the sword added to the racial diversity of the Maghreb.

In the sixteenth century political fragmentation of North Africa made it prey to the expansionism of other Mediterranean powers. Spain established settlements along the coast, defeating local rulers. These in turn called upon the adventurous Barbarossa brothers, who later linked the destinies of the Maghreb to the Ottoman Turks. The establishment of Turkish domination made Algiers an important port for the first time. But the Turkish rule was a turbulent one, marked by assassinations, revolts and massacres.

In the course of the seventeenth century, the Regency of Algiers became increasingly independent of the dictates of the weakening Ottoman Sultan. The Arabs and their Turkish rulers enjoyed the golden age of the Barbary pirates. A number of European states established diplomatic and commercial relations with the Regency. It was not an infrequent occurrence to have a European state seek the assistance of Algiers in a conflict with another European rival.

In the eighteenth century, the Regency declined in prosperity, due largely to a decrease in the influx of pirate booty. Algiers' trade waned and European commercial establishments were reduced in number and importance. As the sea became less profitable, the Turkish rulers turned toward the hinterland to exploit it more fully. This led to increasing dissatisfaction on the part of the Arab tribes and more frequent revolts. The supporters, both military and civilian, of the ruling Deys also became more restless, and assassinations were more frequent.

In the decades just prior to the French conquest, the economic life of the Regency was far from satisfactory for the local inhabitants. The Dey monopolized the sale and set the prices of all imports, and exportation of most local products was forbidden. These uneconomic practices ruined commerce and almost destroyed the agriculture of an otherwise fertile territory. Even in these declining years, pirate tributes were an important part of revenues. Education in the Regency was traditionally Islamic; and science and medicine were little developed. Punishments for crimes were often cruel and procedures inadequate. The Turkish ruling minority held itself aloof and failed to share its power with the local Arabs.

ABD EL KADER AND RURAL RESISTANCE

It was this Government which surrendered to the French expedition on 5 July 1830. Despite lack of sympathy for their Turkish rulers, the Algerians resisted the foreign invasion. From 1830 to 1871, Algerian tribesmen strongly opposed French expansion into the countryside. The French Army of Africa used the most brutal methods in its long pacification campaign. The hero of this era of rural patriotism was Emir Abd El Kader, a young man from Western Algeria, who called upon the Muslims to unite in holy war against the conqueror. This young man, exiled after seventeen years of warfare, is today the popular national hero of Algerian rebels. He worked with poorly trained fighters and primitive weapons, but by his extraordinary energy he succeeded in organizing many if not all of the Algerian tribes.

LAND AND ISLAM

The resistance of Algeria's rural population was not, however, based only on Abd El Kader's leadership and resentment of French brutality. More importantly it was based on Algerian attachment to land and to Islam. French devastation of Muslim lands was extensive, and later confiscations disrupted the basic structure of the rural society. In 1840, a decree provided for confiscation of lands belonging to Algerians who had taken up arms against the French. In 1843, the Turkish Dey's lands and the *habous*[1] were confiscated, thereby giving the French control over Islam. Ordinances of 1844 and 1846 permitted the confiscation of non-developed lands for which no justifiable titles – justifiable under French law – were held before 1830 and the *cantonnement* or restriction of certain tribes to limited areas. These measures not only caused long-lasting and sometimes violent opposition on the part of the population, but confusion as to land-ownership and much litigation.

During the reign of Napoleon III, some effort was made to straighten out the land situation. The *Senatus Consulte* of 1863 declared the tribes to be the rightful owners of lands which they had enjoyed in perpetuity. By providing for various classifications of land, it recognized and established both tribal and individual property rights. Under the decree, *colons* needing land could buy some tribal lands, but not the communally held areas until they were classified as private property. The measure went far toward allaying the fears about *cantonnement*, and attempted gradually to introduce French property concepts. But, some of the boundaries drawn to delimit ownership cut across tribal lines compounding the resentment and resistance.

In 1870, an unsuccessful revolt in Kabylia and in other neighbouring areas led to the confiscation of several million acres of land, a further blow to Algerian rural society. This action impoverished many Kabyles, already among the most resentful of France's new subjects, and sent them to all parts of Algeria in search of work. The Warnier law of 1873 made the *arch* or communal tribal lands available for sale. Land once sold remained thereafter under French land codes and could not return to a previous status under Muslim property law even if bought by a Muslim. Because of the differences between French and Muslim property ownership laws, the land question remains even in the twentieth century a cause of Muslim discontent. The effect of the numerous confiscations was essentially to push the Muslim from the coastal areas and good lands which they had previously owned to the less fertile, less familiar, mountainous hinterland.

During the nineteenth century the primary French institution which dealt with the Algerian tribes was the Arab Bureaux, created in 1844 by General Bugeaud. Officers of the Bureaux had extensive powers, dealt with military and legal matters, collected taxes and engaged in military intelligence activities. The Bureaux persisted with some changes until 1922. The Native Code regulated the status and rights of Algerian Muslims until post-World War I reforms. While objecting to the entire Code, the Algerians were particularly resentful of its restrictions on movements of their flocks and herds through former grazing lands.

The Decline of the Algerian Middle Class[2]

During the era of rural resistance, the Algerian middle class was reduced and dispersed. (It was not reconstituted as such, under French rule, until the early part of this century.) The population of Algiers, estimated at around 75 000 in the eighteenth century was reduced during the first years of the French occupation to about 60 000 of whom only some 25 000 were Muslims. The cities of Blida, Medea, Mascara, Tlemcen, Bône, Constantine and others underwent sieges and massacres during the 1830-47 period, and a large part of the urban population fled to the countryside. Exoduses to the Middle East also occurred throughout the nineteenth century in protest against French measures. The economic troubles of 1854, 1863 and

1868 decreased middle-class wealth; and in 1867, a severe famine took its toll. A particular exception to the history of decline is the city of Constantine, where both religious and political opposition to French rule was to flourish in the last quarter of the nineteenth century. The middle class of the city had ancient origins, high intellectual traditions, an opening on the hinterland and ability to dominate the Turkish ruling class in the cultural field. The Constantine *élite*, supported by the Bey of Constantine, escaped the destruction which the French wrought on other Algerian cities. It is not surprising that Constantine is the home of many Algerian rebel leaders.

During the years prior to 1871, the French made some concessions to Algerians in the political and educational fields. Under Napoleon III, the *Senatus Consulte* of 1865 made Algerians French subjects and permitted them access to the French Army and to minor civil functions. To attain French citizenship, however, the Algerian had to abandon his status under Muslim civil laws, and naturalizations were very few. In the 1880s, certain legislation on behalf of Muslims was enacted in the political field. Most Muslims, however, continued to live in mixed communes administered directly by officials of the French administration.

THE URBANITES SEEK PEACEFUL CHANGE

The crushing of the Kabylia revolt saw the end of the period of rural patriotism and the beginning of efforts by the urban population, led by Constantine, to obtain concessions from the French through peaceful means. In Constantine the religious and political *élites* still remained fused, so opposition to French rule was often couched in religious terms. From 1896 to 1900 the *colons* in Algeria achieved a considerable degree of autonomy, thus making Algeria a separate entity different from the Metropolitan Departments. Thereafter debate was to centre around the status of the Algerian Muslim in an already unique Algeria, where the two communities did not share the same French rights. Under the Financial Delegations, Algerians were to receive a representation of one-third. However, only two

Algerians were appointed in the early period and these from the wealthy landowning class. It was not until 1922 that twenty-one Muslims were appointed to the Delegations; in 1937 their number was raised to twenty-four. In any case, the minority representation of the Algerians on the Delegations left them with little actual power.

THE YOUNG ALGERIAN PARTY

In 1907 another revolt was suppressed, and in 1911 the administration put down demonstrations against the results of rigged elections. About this time, the first, if very short-lived, Algerian party was formed. Called the *Young Algerian Party*, it accepted the newly created obligation of Muslims to do military service for France but requested increased Muslim representation in elected assemblies, the development of education and the end of special Arab taxes and of the Native Code.

In 1911, some 800 residents of Tlemcen decided to leave the city and emigrate to Syria. The causes of discontent were many and the exodus showed the apparent sense of futility on the part of this group at least to attempt to work out its difficulties within the framework of the existing French régime.[3]

ALGERIAN MIGRATION

Even before the First World War some Algerians from poor rural areas had emigrated to France in search of work. However, it was the war which gave impetus to a truly mass migration. From an estimated 4–5000, the number of Algerians working in France during the war rose to about 80 000. Migration to France continued up to 1924 to fill France's reconstruction manpower needs. After 1924 it dropped sharply, as it did again in 1929 with the advent of the world economic depression. In 1936, when migration again began, the number of Algerians working in France was estimated at 32 000, to be compared with about 100 000 who came to work between 1920 and 1924. During the Second World War little migration of Algerian workers occurred. After 1946, however, France again had need of manpower and by 1954 some 3–400 000 Algerians were working in France.

CLEMENCEAU'S REFORMS

The efforts and sacrifices of Algerian workers and soldiers during the First World War and obvious discontent in Algeria led the French Left to favour reforms. Premier Clemenceau refused to yield to *colon* objections to a series of mild proposals. In 1919, therefore, a law provided that educated Algerians could obtain French citizenship if they abandoned their personal status under Muslim civil laws. (The *Senatus Consulte* of 1865 had made this possible much earlier, but under such complex procedures that naturalization was most unlikely.) Few Algerians responded, however, and by 1936 only a few thousand had been naturalized. The reforms also ended the special Arab taxes; gave Algerians one-fourth of the seats on the General Councils of the Algerian Departments; and permitted Algerian members of Municipal Councils to vote in the elections for mayors.

THE BLUM-VIOLETTE PROPOSAL

Algerians who had achieved a degree of French education soon began to demand that they be accepted as French citizens despite their Muslim civil status. These moderates sought a new type of assimilation: a more equal status within Algerian society. In the elections of May 1936, the French Left achieved a substantial victory and a Popular Front Government was formed under the leadership of Socialist Léon Blum. Responding to calls of the Algerian moderates, the government favoured the proposed Blum-Violette law which would have granted French citizenship to certain categories of educated Muslims in Algeria without abandonment of Muslim status. The Blum-Violette proposal was not approved by the French Parliament because of strong *colon* opposition. Its failure led to the disillusionment of many educated Algerians who were devoted to French culture.

THE 1944 ORDINANCE

During the Second World War, Algerians again fought in large numbers on behalf of France. They did so although

French and Allied authorities landing in North Africa in late 1942 failed to respond to demands for reforms by a unified Algerian nationalistic *élite*. It was not until March 1944 that an Ordinance promulgated by General de Gaulle declared certain categories of Muslims, similar to those in the Blum-Violette proposal, to be French citizens. The Ordinance also abolished many special laws concerning Muslims and increased Muslim representation in local assemblies from one-third to two-fifths, in General Councils from one-quarter to two-fifths and in the Assembly which replaced the Financial Delegations, from one-third to half. By the Lamine-Gueye law of May 1946, French citizenship was granted to inhabitants of all overseas territories including those of Algeria. Thus for the first time all Algerians enjoyed equal legal status with the European *colons*.

THE STATUTE OF 1947

Despite the Algerian revolt of 1945, Algerians participated in the elections for the first and second French Constituent Assemblies and voted on the French Constitution of October 1946. This Constitution ended the 'Régime of Decrees' which had ruled Algeria since 1830. Under the Constitution, Algeria was one of several Overseas Departments where the same legislation as that of Metropolitan France would apply except as provided in laws passed by the French Assembly itself. The compatibility of personal religious status with French citizenship was proclaimed in Article 82 of the Constitution.

It was not until 1947 that the French National Assembly considered special legislation for Algeria. As earlier, the Algerians found that they had little power to influence the formulation of the new law. Their proposals were rejected and they refused to participate in the final vote. The Statute of Algeria as it emerged was a compromise between the French Left and *colon* pressure – forces which so often before had determined the direction of Algerian affairs.

The Statute of 1947 proclaimed that Algeria 'constitutes a group of departments endowed with a civil personality, financial autonomy and a particular organization . . .'. It declared the 'effective equality of all French citizens'. All those of French nationality in the Algerian Departments were to enjoy the rights and obligations of French citizenship without distinction of origin, race, language or religion. Under the Statute, the Governor-General, the Council of Government and the Algerian Assembly governed Algeria. The Assembly was composed of 120 members, of whom sixty were elected by the first college of *colons* and certain educated Muslims, and sixty by the second college of the remaining Muslims. The legislative régime for Algeria was a complex one with certain French laws made directly applicable to Algeria and power to legislate in certain vital spheres given exclusively to the French Parliament. Some existing laws and future laws in limited fields could be considered or modified for Algeria by the Algerian Assembly. If the Governor-General refused to promulgate a law of the Assembly, as required by the Statute, the final decision rested with the French Parliament. The decisions of the Assembly were taken by a majority vote, although a two-thirds majority might be required at the request either of the Governor-General, the Commission of Finance or one-quarter of the Assembly's members. The Assembly voted on the Algerian budget drawn up by the Governor-General, although a balanced budget had to be assured.

The Algerian Assembly was the first governmental institution in Algeria in which Algerians were given sizeable representation, but its inequities were clear. The electoral list of March 1954 showed 500 000 European voters along with 70 000 Muslims in the first college and some 1 450 000 Muslim voters in the second college. (This figure did not include any Muslim women.) However, the inequality of representation is even more striking when the population as a whole is considered. Such a comparison shows one European vote equal to about nine Muslim votes. It may also be observed that the provision for a two-thirds vote, which could easily be invoked permitted the *colons* to dominate the legislative process by an effective veto. Furthermore, the principal liberal provisions of the Statute were dependent upon action by the Algerian Assembly.

These included the extension of the right to vote to Muslim women; the end of Mixed Communes; administration of localities by Councils elected by secret and direct universal vote; separation of Islam from the French State; and the teaching of Arabic at all levels. In practice, also, the elections which took place for the Assembly were widely rigged, bringing to that body for the most part administration-supported candidates. The real locus of power under the 1947 Statute still rested in the hands of the Governor-General and the French Government of which he was the sole representative in Algeria. Algeria remained under the régime of the Statute until the outbreak of the rebellion. Thereafter special emergency legislation, eventually applied to all Algeria, prevailed. The Algerian Assembly was finally dissolved in 1956.

The Psychology of the Algerian

If the Statute of 1947 proclaimed the Algerian equal to the European *colon*, it did not make him so either in fact or in law. It did not remove the many traces on his personality of the French colonial system. To the Algerian, the essential fact of that system is discrimination – against his culture and language, against him personally and collectively in every field. That discrimination is backed by the power of the French Army, exercised so brutally as recently as 1945. In part because of discrimination and force, the twentieth-century Algerian had in some cases become that colonial stereotype: uneducated, unemployed, unkempt, unambitious, psychologically hostile. The crushing out of the Algerian personality was increasingly resented by the educated Algerian, who was never fully accepted by France. At the same time the individual member of the *élite* found himself drawing farther and farther away from the Algerian of the village. Culturally, the Algerian was torn between an awakening Arab-Muslim world and the West, and often possessed a resultant inferiority complex. His protests against his status tended to be violent – both verbally and physically – because more evolutionary means were not open to him or he was ignorant of their use. On the Algerian political scene, he was frustrated by his lack of knowledge of ways which were essentially foreign to him and by lack of support similar to that received from France by the *colons*. Economically, the Algerian was depressed, often living on the subsistence level and sometimes below. He therefore possessed neither the economic means to achieve political power, nor even the financial means to escape his crushing burdens. Every Algerian was in this context a latent rebel.

The rebellion has profoundly changed the psychological outlook of the Algerian. Even the poorest peasant was given an Army and a Provisional Government that made his second-class status no longer seem significant. Through its own propaganda efforts, the rebel leadership has instilled a new sense of 'belonging' in its followers and a new respect for their hitherto submerged heritage. French contentions that the Algerian could not be trained in technical and administrative skills, that he was lazy and irrational – all have been progressively disproved, with a corresponding rise in Algerian morale. This does not mean that traces on the Algerian personality of the long period of colonialism have disappeared. Ultra-sensitivity is still there – but the colonial imprint is undergoing a striking transformation.

REFERENCES

1 The habous were lands or other donations made in perpetuity to the Muslim cult. The incomes derived therefrom supported the mosques, Muslim officials and other religious activities, thus permitting the independence of Islam.

2 For the general analysis of this section, I have relied on Lacheraf, 'Le Nationalisme Algérien: Sens d'une Revolution', *Les Temps Modernes*, September-October 1956.

3 Among the objections were: military conscription which forced Muslims to serve under the flag of infidels; the confiscation of *habous*; proposals to place buildings under French property law contrary to the Muslim code; the Native Code; required travel permits; inequities in the functions of the courts; increased taxes; insufficient representation of Algerians in elected assemblies; economic transformations which ruined local activities, notably the competition of European manufacturers which ruined small Algerian industries; the superiority of the Jews over the Muslims; sabotage of teaching by the assemblies with the aid of the academic authorities; the increasing rigours of the forestry régime; the difficulties and penalties of the customs; the heavy taxes in the villages and the often inexact and inequitable way they were established; the protection accorded by administrators to their subordinates even when they committed abuses, and the complete absence of control on the part of the Prefects and the Governor-General with regard to complaints of the Algerians. The data taken from the Report of the Commission of Inquiry is cited in Julien *L'Afrique du Nord en Marche*, pp. 104-5.

Chapter 3

1954: The *Colon* and the Algerian

THE POPULATION

THE STATUS of the two distinct communities in Algeria in 1954 is closely connected with the rebellion which broke out on the night of 31 October–1 November of that year. Within a short period and continuing into 1959, the rebel leadership had received the tacit co-operation, if not active participation, of many Algerian Muslims. The reason for this support may lie in the degree of failure of communication between the *colons* and the Algerians. This failure is the result of different geographic locations, different economic wealth and pursuits, different educational levels and cultural outlooks. The official census taken in Algeria in October 1948, the first in the post-war years, showed a total population of 8 682 000, of which 7 708 000 were Muslims and 974 000 were Europeans. The official census of 1954 showed an increase to a total of 9 528 000, of which some 8 486 000 were Muslims and 1 042 000 Europeans. But the Muslim population may have been underestimated for political reasons. The population was located primarily in the fertile coastal region, which makes up only one-tenth of the whole territory. The highest concentration of population was in the central Algiers Department; the lowest in the western Oran Department. The vast Southern Territories of the Sahara counted less than one person per square mile. The ratio of Muslims to Europeans in the eastern Department of Constantine was the highest of the three Departments, amounting to about 18 to 1. This, along with the facility of access to Algeria over the mountainous Algerian-Tunisian border and Constantine's long traditions, may account for the selection of eastern Algeria as the first target area of the rebellion. In Oran, which remained peaceful for many months after November 1954, the Muslim-European ratio was only about 5 to 1.

URBANIZATION

Large migratory movements of the population both within Algeria and between Algeria and Metropolitan France have taken place in recent years. Although Algeria remains essentially an agricultural country, its urban population increased more than fourfold between 1886 and 1954. In the same period, the rural population increased less than twofold. This trend toward urbanization existed among both Muslims and Europeans. However, it was more striking on the part of the Europeans, 80% of whom lived in cities in 1954, whereas only 64% did so in 1886. Muslims have also tended to move to the city in the past century. In 1886, only 7% of them lived in cities, while 18% did so in 1954. Not all of these Algerians can be said to participate in urban life as do the Europeans. Many of the Muslims have found housing only in tin can shanty towns. Others have had to cross the Mediterranean to France before finding work and lodging. In 1948, there were about 160 000 Algerians in France, increasing to about 400 000 in 1955. The effects of Muslim migration to the principal cities of Algeria are striking. In Constantine, the Muslim population has always outnumbered the European, but it did so only by a margin of about 6000 in 1886. In 1954, it did so by some 62 000. In Bône, another principal city of eastern Algeria and an important port, Europeans outnumbered Muslims, only until 1948. In Algiers, Muslims outnumbered non-Muslims for the first time in 1954. In the city of Oran, the European population has always outnumbered the Muslim, but the latter has proportionately increased. Thus, in 1886 Europeans outnumbered Muslims in three of four principal cities in Algeria while in 1954 the situation was reversed and Europeans remained in a majority only in Oran. These facts are of considerable import for those who have thought a partition might be a viable solution for Algeria.

NATIONAL ORIGINS

While all inhabitants of Algeria were French citizens in 1954, the ethnic composition of the two populations reflected the many migrations of the preceding centuries. Of the 'European' population of just over 1 000 000 in that year, 140–150 000 were Jews of North African, Italian or Spanish origin. Of the remainder, about 50% were of French origin, or about 450 000. These are the only *colons* who would have a real ethnic claim to return to France should independence be granted – a much smaller number than usually publicized. The remaining Europeans were largely of Spanish, Italian and Maltese origin. The law of 1889 automatically naturalized children born in Algeria of foreign parents. By 1954, only about 5% of the European population did not have French citizenship. Most of the Europeans of all origins were born in Algeria and only 11% were born elsewhere. These were mostly from Metropolitan France and came to Algeria as members of the administration, or as industrialists, or professional men.

POPULATION STRUCTURE

The demographic structure of the Europeans of Algeria reveals them to be a young population. In 1954, about 11% of this group was over 60 years of age. In the under-20 age group, there were about 35%, and 54% were between 20 and 60 years old. The rate of increase of the European population is about 1% per year, resulting from a fairly stable birth-rate since 1939 and a steady decrease in the death-rate. Infant mortality which was 94 for each 1000 live births in 1939 decreased sharply to 45 in 1955. The birth-rate of the European population is none the less somewhat lower than in Metropolitan France and mortality, especially infant mortality, is higher.

While the structure of the European population is comparatively young, the Muslim population is one of the youngest and most rapidly increasing in the world. In 1954, over 50% of the population was under 20 years of age: an indication of an immense school problem. About 5% of all Muslims were over 60 years of age, and the remaining 45% were between 20 and

60. The annual rate of increase of the population in 1954 was 2·5%. The Muslim population rapidly increased during the period of French occupation, notably after 1870. It was about 2·5 million in 1876, 4·7 million in 1901, and 5·7 million in 1921. At the present rate the Muslims will about double their numbers again by 1980. The rapid rise of the Muslim population in the post-World War II period is the focal point of many of Algeria's economic problems, and has made the Algerian peasant even more unfortunate than he was in 1939. He has found himself squeezed between his meagre resources and many new mouths to feed. Migration has helped somewhat; and about 2 000 000 Algerians are supported by relatives working in Metropolitan France. But the population 'explosion' has also furnished the increasing ranks of the unemployed and many recruits for the rebel army.

DISTRIBUTION OF THE LABOUR FORCE

Another index of the relative positions of the two communities living in Algeria is that of Muslim and European participation in the different sectors of the economy. In 1954, 75% of the active population was engaged in agriculture. Of these, Muslims formed the overwhelming majority. The next largest group of Muslims were engaged in mining, processing industries and power, where they made up 62% of the total. A third large category of Muslims, again the overwhelming majority, were working as non-agricultural day labourers. Muslims represented 61% of those engaged in commerce. In the category of administration and services there were some 73 000 Muslims out of a total of 157 000. The census listed some 54 000 unemployed Muslims out of a total of 68 000. This assessment, made for the first time in 1954, did not reveal the true extent of unemployment and under-employment among Muslims. In the agricultural sector, estimates of under-employment ran as high as 800 000. In all sectors, there were about 900 000 unemployed and under-employed out of a total active population of 3 500 000, or about one-fourth of the total Muslim labour force. Every reform proposal for Algeria has included the creation of new jobs. De Gaulle's 1958 Constantine programme proposed 400 000 new positions in the next five years – highly inadequate if measured against present unemployment of over 1 000 000.

The *colon* labour force was much more equally divided between the agricultural and non-agricultural sectors of the economy. The largest number of Europeans, 106 000, were found in mining, power and processing industries. In the administration and services, there were about 84 000 Europeans in 1954. In commerce, there were about 64 000, while there were only some 32 000 engaged in agriculture. The census showed some 14 000 unemployed Europeans. However, many of these persons either did not choose to work or had income from other sources.

LAND-OWNERSHIP AND INCOME DISTRIBUTION

The poverty of the vast majority of Algerians results not only from the fact of a high percentage of permanent unemployment, but also from concentration of both land and industrial wealth in the hands of the *colons*. Following the outbreak of the rebellion, studies were undertaken of the Algerian economic crisis, which many believed to be at the root of the problem. One such study, made for the French Economic Council by Mr. Robert Delavignette in July 1955, showed an extremely inequitable division of cultivable land in Algeria. According to Delavignette's Report, of about 15 000 000 acres of cultivable land, European owners, 25 000 in number, owned 6 875 000 acres. This gave each European farmer 275 acres on the average. Also in the modern agricultural sector were some 15 000 Muslim farm owners possessing 1 875 000 acres, averaging 150 acres per farm. The vast majority of Muslim owners were concentrated in the traditional agricultural sector. Five hundred thousand Muslim owners possessed some 6 250 000 acres, thus averaging only 12·5 acres per farm. Not only did Europeans have farms many times larger than those of Muslims, but they also owned the most fertile lands where the most valuable crops were grown.

For example, Europeans owned virtually all vineyards, while Muslims were predominant in wheat growing – a crop yielding a much lower income per acre.

Another study, made on the financial relations between Algeria and Metropolitan France by M. Maspétiol in June 1955, showed that the vast majority of Algerian Muslims had an average annual income of only about $45. And only some 50 000 Muslims earned as much as $502 a year. On the other hand, no Europeans were in the two lowest classes of the population and none earned less than $240 a year. Some 15 000 'top crust' Europeans earned $3181 a year. Maspétiol divided the Muslim and European populations of Algeria into five distinct classes, as follows:

ALGERIAN POPULATION CLASSES AND INCOMES, 1951

Income per person[1]	Muslim	European	Total	Class
$45	5 840 000	—	5 840 000	Traditional agriculture
$121	1 600 000	—	1 600 000	Urban Muslims
$240	510 000	440 000	950 000	Small and medium wage-earners, craftsmen and businessmen
$502	50 000	545 000	595 000	Middle class
$3181		15 000	15 000	Wealthy class
	8 000 000	1 000 000	9 000 000	Total

Adapted from: France, Government-General of Algeria, *Rapport du Groupe d'Etude des Relations Financières entre la Metropole et l'Algérie* June 1955, pp. 79, 80.

One of the inequities to which Maspétiol paid particular attention was that of the different tax burdens on the various classes of the population. The relatively slight graduation in the tax burden has tended to favour the wealthier classes. In 1951, the burden ranged from 12·7% for the class of Muslims earning $45 a year to only 29·2% for the wealthy *colons* earning $3181. Urban Muslims earning only $121 a year had about the same burden (20·4%) as middle-class Europeans (21·4%) earning $502 a year.

Another factor contributing to the poverty of Algeria's Muslims was the extremely low salary rates in both agriculture and industry. The Delavignette Report noted that minimum hourly industrial wages in Algeria in October 1954 ranged from 74 francs to 91 francs (about 27 cents). In France the vast majority of workers received 121½ francs. In April 1955 a new decree slightly raised these minimum wages. Agricultural salaries were also extremely low. In October 1954, an agricultural worker received between 317 and 407 francs *per day*. By comparison, agricultural salaries in France ranged from 853–1059 francs per day. Agricultural wages were also slightly increased in April 1955. The agricultural sector had other disadvantages for the vast majority of Muslims employed there: long hours, bad conditions and employment for only part of the year. Discrimination against Algerians in fringe benefits also occurred, and salaries in both agriculture and industry did not keep pace with rising cost of living in the five years preceding the rebellion.

LITERACY AND ILLITERACY

The economic poverty of the Algerian Muslim is both the reflection and in some measure the cause of his lack of education. France failed to spend sufficient sums to permit the increasing number of Algerian children to go to school in the post-war years. The census of 1948 showed that only 9% of Muslim males and 2·1% of females could write any language. In 1954, illiteracy was still well above 90%. In contrast, the vast majority of Europeans were literate. All European children desiring education were in schools that year, while only 15–20% of Muslim children were able to attend. Over 2 000 000 Muslim children of school age were without schooling. Only some 500–600 Muslims were attending the University of Algiers, out of a total student body of over 5000. Muslim attendance, therefore, at Algerian institutions of higher learning amounted approximately to 0·0066% of its population, as compared with 0·45% among Europeans, 0·3% in France, and 1·8% in the United States.[2] In France, there was about one student in higher education for every 300 inhabitants. In Algeria, there was one European student for every 227

Europeans and one Muslim student for every 15 342 Muslims. Similar disparities occurred at all levels of education.

ALGERIA: RAW MATERIALS AND CHEAP LABOUR

The industrialization which might have improved the Algerian economic situation despite Muslim population increases had been barely started by 1954. The reasons for this are diverse, but connected at many points with what has been called the 'colonial economic compact'. The customs union between Algeria and France made it difficult to establish any industry in competition with French manufacturing. The shipping monopoly, which permitted certain French maritime companies to control a large part of the transportation between Algeria and France increased the costs of any would-be Algerian industrialist. The high price of power was also discouraging. Until the recent Saharan discoveries, Algeria has lacked vital fuels. The nature of the tax system, unfavourable to industry, was a further hindrance. But perhaps the main reason that Algeria has remained essentially an exporter of agricultural products and unprocessed minerals is the financial interests of its wealthy *colons*. While investing in various industries in France, they have gained their fortunes in Algeria from vast acres producing grapes, fine grasses, tobacco, cotton and ore. These powerful men and a few banking and investment corporations 'own' Algeria, and have thus far not found it in their economic interest to industrialize rapidly. This has not prevented the French Government from drawing up several plans for increased industrialization, but by 1954 such projects had done little to lessen the economic poverty and unemployment of the Algerian Muslim. This, along with his political frustrations, served to make him a willing follower of nationalists seeking independence, greater economic welfare and personal dignity.

REFERENCES

[1] At the official 1951 exchange rate of 350 francs to $1.
[2] The percentage figures are based on the following rough divisions; 600/9 000 000 for Algerian Muslim; 150 000/43 000 000 for France; 3 000 000/160 000 000 for the United States; and 5400/1 200 000 for Algerian Europeans.

PART II

ALGERIAN RESPONSE WITHIN THE FRENCH SYSTEM

Chapter 4

The Beginnings of Nationalism

ALGERIAN nationalism is unique among modern national-
isms, even among those now existing or taking shape
in the neighbouring Middle East and Africa. Unlike the
nationalists elsewhere, Algerians made their first important
demands for change within the framework of the French State
and French political parties. It may even be said that Algerian
nationalism, in the sense of 'a living and active corporate will'
to independence and an overriding loyalty of any large number
of Algerians to that goal, is a product rather than a cause of
the 1954 rebellion. This is not to assert that Algeria has not
formed a distinct ethnic, cultural, economic and sometimes
political entity for many centuries. But the average Algerian
peasant probably had little awareness of his national identity
until the present revolution channelled his discontent arising
from poverty and cultural repression and gave him both a
concrete goal and the means, albeit at great sacrifice, to
achieve it.

THE BLOC OF ELECTED ALGERIAN MUSLIMS

The Clemenceau reforms of 1919 and the great changes brought
about by World War I inspired political activities among urban
Algerian Muslims. The most important leader of this group
was Emir Khaled, grandson of the nineteenth-century hero,
Abd El Kader. He sought unsuccessfully to unite rural resistance, which had steadily declined since 1871, with a nascent
urban patriotism. His short-lived *Bloc of Algerian Elected
Muslims* exposed the excesses of the French administration and

attacked the feudalism of both the *colons* and the French-appointed Muslim religious officials. Emir Khaled's demands for justice went largely unheeded, however, and he was banished by the French in 1924.

THE NORTH AFRICAN STAR AND THE PARTY OF THE ALGERIAN PEOPLE

During the early 1920s, lack of employment opportunity and France's reconstruction needs brought many young Algerians there to find work. One such migrant was Messali Ahmed Ben Hadj, who later came to be called the 'Father of Algerian Nationalism' and on whose personal energies and bents the course of that nationalism was in large part to depend. Messali was born in 1898 in Tlemcen – the city of the mass exodus of 1911. The son of a poor shoemaker, the young Messali had little education. He fought in the First World War in the French Army, returning to Algeria in 1921. Unable to find work, he went back to France about 1923, where he held a number of jobs in Paris factories, and was a street vendor for a time. He took courses at the School of Oriental Languages and attended lectures at the University of Bordeaux. Like many other Algerian workers, he lived under extremely adverse conditions and identified himself with the struggling French working class. He soon joined the Communist Party, and later married a French Communist. His experience in the Paris Communist cells gave him a pattern of organization which he later impressed upon the Algerian national movement.

In 1925-6, Messali created the *Etoile Nord Africaine* (ENA) – the North African Star – dedicated to the defence of 'the material, moral and social interests of North African Muslims'. In 1927, he became the President of the ENA and gradually lessened its early ties with the Communist Party. The ENA demanded from the first independence for all North Africa, representing Tunisian and Moroccan workers in Paris as well as Algerians. The North African idea was to crop up again and again in the course of the Algerian national movement. But Algerian workers soon dominated the ENA and the attention of the Tunisians and Moroccans was turned toward internal events in their respective countries. Other than the general aim of independence, the early militants of the ENA had only a vague doctrine, which has been described as 'a surface Marxism, a nostalgic and sentimental Algerianism, a summary Islamism'.[1]

The ENA was dissolved by the French Government in 1929 for its demands for independence. Many of its members went underground, thus incidentally reinforcing the Communist organizational pattern which they had earlier adopted. In that same year, the *Glorious Star* was formed with less strident demands and a moderate programme designed to repudiate the French 'civilizing mission' in Algeria. About this time the party workers began to publish *El Ouma* (The Nation). This newspaper appeared sporadically and, like the militants themselves, was often the victim of French repressive measures.

In 1933, the ENA again reappeared and held an important General Assembly meeting in France. Messali and his followers passed a long resolution containing demands for measures to be taken both before and after independence.[2] Their wide scope reflected not only the Communist influence upon the movement, but also the quite utopian and theoretical framework of the few devoted militants in the early 1930s. If total independence was not startling enough for the French, the provision concerning eventual confiscation of large properties in Algeria made it almost certain that the authorities would reject the ENA demands outright.

While the activities of the ENA were confined largely to France, contact was also maintained with Tunisians, Moroccans and other Arab and Islamic groups. In 1927, Messali attended the anti-imperialist congress in Belgium which had such an influence on the minds of many Asian and African nationalists. In 1930, he sent a memorandum to the League of Nations asking its help in achieving ENA aims.

In 1934, the ENA was started up for a second time under the name of the *National Union of North African Muslims*. This group still included all of North Africa within its scope and took part in many of the French working-class battles of the era. In the same year Messali was imprisoned on the charge, frequently used against him and other nationalists, of 'reconstituting a dissolved organization'. After his release from prison in the spring of 1935 he continued his agitation, and notably took part in the campaign against the Italian invasion of Ethiopia. Only a few months after his release, Messali was again subject to arrest, under the harsh Regnier Decree. To avoid prison, he spent six months' self-imposed exile in Switzerland. There his horizons were broadened at the Muslim Congress in Geneva and by his contacts with Chekib Arslan, Lebanese savant and 'Father' of Pan-Arabism and Pan-Islamism in the Middle East. This unusual visionary is credited with turning Messali from a Communist-French orientation toward Arabism and Islam. He influenced the young Algerian to oppose the assimilationist Blum-Violette proposal and to increase his contact with the reformist Islamic movement in Algeria.

The coming of the Popular Front Government in France permitted Messali's return to Paris, where he again took up his organizational and propaganda activities. On Bastille Day, 1936, some 40 000 North African workers paraded in Paris demanding the liberation of the whole Arab world. Messali and the ENA made their first entry into Algeria proper on 2 August at a mass meeting of 10 000 Algerians at the Municipal Stadium of Algiers. Thereafter Messali toured Algeria giving a series of speeches with special success in his native Tlemcen region. At this time the ENA claimed to have 11 000 members organized into seven sections in France and some thirty sections, recently founded in Algeria. An additional thirty-one sections of the organization were started during Messali's trip. Messali's campaign against the Blum-Violette proposal and for independence was opposed by the assimilationist Algerian Muslim Congress and the Communist Party, which as a French Government party favoured continued French sovereignty. This dispute had two important repercussions: the abandonment by many Algerians of their Communist ties in favour of the nationalist ENA and the dissolution of the ENA by the Popular Front Government in January 1937.

On 11 March 1937 Messali founded in France the *Parti du Peuple Algérien* (PPA) – the Party of the Algerian People – having the same general demands as the ENA, but in an entirely Algerian framework. The party still found its basic support in Algerian worker circles in France. In June, Messali returned to Algeria and the PPA sponsored its first candidates for the Algiers municipal election. Shortly thereafter, the PPA chief was again arrested for 'exhortation to acts of disorder against the sovereignty of the State' and sentenced to two years in prison with deprivation of political and civil rights. But the imprisonment of Messali, Lahouel and other PPA leaders did not prevent their election to the Municipal Council – a testimony to the strong feelings which Messali's sojourn in Algeria had aroused. Messali was free for a few months in 1939, but in September the PPA was again dissolved and its current newspaper, *Le Parlement Algérien* (The Algerian Parliament), suppressed. Messali, along with Lahouel, Khider and Mezerna, was again arrested; and finally, in March 1941, he was sentenced by the Vichy Government to sixteen years of forced labour and twenty years of exclusion from Algeria. He had refused collaboration with the Pétain régime.

In the fifteen years of its existence prior to 1940, the Algerian national movement led by Messali had undergone considerable evolution. It had given up its initial ties with the Communist Party of France, while accepting the basic organizational pattern of that party. It had also abandoned, although only temporarily, links with other North Africans in the struggle against France for independence. The decision to form the PPA on a purely Algerian basis was a tactical one, dictated by the legal structure which made Algeria a part of France, and made Tunisia and Morocco protectorates. The PPA had also evolved from a party concerned largely with betterment of the lot of the Algerian worker in France to activity in the wider context of Algeria itself and Algerian independence. In 1940, the strength of the PPA still remained in France. The party had developed a small press and its militants had achieved a certain degree of experience in political and propaganda activity. It is in this sphere that Messali and the PPA have been criticized for intransigence, improvisation and absence of a well-thought-out doctrine.[3] These shortcomings may well reflect the generally low calibre of the militants, their low economic status and their lack of education. In any case, the ENA-PPA did introduce the idea of independence which became the cornerstone of subsequent political development among Algerian Muslims. The PPA had little or no realistic methodology outlined for the achievement of that independence; and the era was in fact not ripe for such rapid evolution. That the PPA survived at all despite frequent and extensive arrests and repressive measures, as well as the confiscation of its newspapers, is a commentary on the strength of the very idea of independence. Mixed with this central theme were suggestions of fraternity and solidarity with North Africa as a whole and Arab and Islamic worlds. But the strand of proletarianism was perhaps stronger, and when PPA militants set out specific demands they did so in the terms of the workers of the French Left. By 1940, however, a certain disillusion with the assistance which might come to Algerian nationalism from the Left had set in, and younger party members were to be more influenced by the fall of France in 1940 than by the idea of co-operation.

THE ALGERIAN SOCIETY OF REFORMIST ULEMA

After the exile of Emir Khaled in 1924, nationalist activities were considerably reduced in Algeria. In the decade of the 1930s, support for Algerian nationalism came from religious quarters through the establishment in 1931 of the *Society of Reformist Ulema*. The *Ulema* (Doctors of Muslim Law) took their inspiration from the Salafiya and Wahabist movements in the Middle East and from the modern Egyptian reformist doctrine of Sheik Mohamed Abdo.[4] It was this Islamic education that Algerian Sheik Abdelhamid Ben Badis received when he attended the Islamic Zitouna University in Tunis. Ben Badis, who has been called the 'strongest personality of Maghrebian Islam', impressed his views on the group of Constantine intellectuals and savants who formed the Society of Reformist *Ulema*. Two of Ben Badis' collaborators, Sheiks El Okbi and Ibrahimi, also had an important influence on the *Ulema*. From Constantine these three men directed an extensive campaign to modernize Algerian Muslim practices. Ben Badis edited a monthly magazine entitled *The Vision of the Future*, in addition to writing frequently for the magazine published by Chekib Arslan, *The Arab Nation*.

The doctrine of the *Ulema* was primarily a religious one, but its political overtones served to awaken nationalist feelings in the Algerian masses. In 1938, Ben Badis asserted:

> Islam is the religion of God and must be, *par excellence*, that of Humanity. It honours and glorifies reason and recommends that all acts of life be based on reasoning. It condemns the servitude of man to man, as well as despotism in all its forms . . . it is essentially democratic and does not admit absolutism at all, even for the benefit of the most just man.

The doctrines of the *Ulema* were little short of revolutionary. In 1936, when assimilationists were calling for tighter links between Algeria and France and greater participation of Algerians in French political and cultural life, Ben Badis declared: 'The Algerian people is not France, and does not wish to be France, and even if it wished, it could not be, for it is a people very far from France by its language, its customs, its origin and its religion.' In 1937, he wrote in *The Vision of the Future*: 'Islam is a social system which responds to all the needs of life, in all countries, at all times. Only its principles can permit Humanity to build its happiness.' In 1938, he strongly attacked French naturalization for Muslims: 'Naturalization – that is, the option of a Muslim for a people which is not Muslim – includes the rejection of the divine laws which regulate him and the adoption of human and profane laws. . . .' He concluded:

> The first fruit of our propaganda will be the end of assimilation in fact, which is that of certain ignoble functionaries . . . who harm *Islam* and *Arabism* to please the

authorities. It will also lead to *the end of that other spiritual assimilation* which is that of certain Europeanized [persons] ignorant of the nobility of their race . . . to the point that one can no longer distinguish them from their masters.[5]

To carry out their reformation in Algeria, the *Ulema* created societies, circles – some even in Metropolitan France among workers – and private mosques. More importantly, they established a number of primary Koranic schools and gave courses in several cities on Islamic philosophy, law, practices, history and other subjects, including the basic teaching of Arabic. They also encouraged many of their students to attend the Zitouna, El Azhar, in Cairo and other universities in the Arab world for higher training. Children in the primary schools run by the *Ulema* began their day by chanting in unison: 'Islam is my religion, Arabic is my language, Algeria is my country.' The *Ulema* demanded the right to preach in the mosques in competition with the French-appointed religious hierarchy. Their principal aim was the complete separation of the Muslim cult from French State control.

The demands of the *Ulema*, both religious and cultural, brought them into conflict with the French administration, and resulted in strong measures against them. In 1930, the administration instituted Consultative Committees of the Cult in each Department, a step of doubtful legality since France had promised not to interfere with Islam in the Treaty of 1830. In 1933, local authorities were ordered to keep a watch on Communist agents and the *Ulema*, both considered suspect of danger to the French cause. Several decrees gave the French-appointed religious officials monopoly of preaching in the mosques, and made a Frenchman President of the Consultative Council of the Cult. The appointment of a French Christian was particularly resented, as it placed a non-Muslim and an administration official in direct control of religious affairs. But *Ulema* propaganda was still carried to the Algerian masses – an effort which was particularly successful due to its religious origin. The high prestige of the *Ulema* declined somewhat with the death in 1940 of their extraordinarily gifted leader, Ben Badis. As a group, the *Ulema* did not take a direct part in Algerian politics either before or after the Second World War, but their support was often sought by one or the other of the competing political groups. Their demands for an Islamic renaissance, the use of Arabic and for separation of the cult from the State have been espoused by all Algerian nationalists.

THE FEDERATION OF ELECTED MUSLIMS

The radical demands of Messali's followers and the conservative reformation favoured by the *Ulema* did not touch to any great extent the Westernized and educated Muslim *élite* which was beginning to form in the decades after World War I. This *élite* contented itself for the most part with educational and financial achievements. It had, however, in Ferhat Abbas, a pharmacist living in Sétif, an eloquent spokesman. In his *The Young Algerian*, published in 1931, Abbas asserted: 'Algeria is French territory. We are Frenchmen with Muslim personal status.' His theme, that of progressing 'from a colony toward a province' well expressed the assimilationist desires of certain intellectuals. To achieve this goal, however, 'colonization' must end. 'There is nothing', he wrote, 'in the *Holy Book* which could prevent a Muslim Algerian from being nationally a Frenchman with *strong arms, and awakened intelligence, a loyal heart,* conscious of national solidarity. There is nothing except colonization.' In *The Young Algerian* Abbas expresses a strong sensitivity to French criticism of Westernized Algerians and of Islam; a desire to reject the Turkish responsibility for the decadence of Algeria by creating a more ancient picture of his country; resentment of Jews and other assimilated foreigners for placing themselves between France and the Algerians; a refusal to analyse profoundly the social questions of the day and the Socialist and Communist problem; a courteous criticism of French policy and an ardent defence of Muslim civilization.[6]

In 1930, those of the *élite* who had represented Muslims in local elected bodies formed the *Federation of Elected Muslims*, led by Dr. Bendjelloul, who headed the Constantine group. The principal doctrine of this somewhat heterogeneous association was the gradual integration of the Muslim *élite* into French life and the bettering of conditions for all Muslims in Algeria.[7] In 1935, Ferhat Abbas, speaking on behalf of the Federation, told visiting French Minister of the Interior Regnier: 'there is nothing left in this country but the way of assimilation, of fusion of the native element in French society'. The following year, Abbas made his position even more clear in his oft-quoted statement:

> We, political friends of Dr. Bendjelloul, we would be nationalists. The accusation is not new. I have talked with diverse personalities about this question. My opinion is known: nationalism is that sentiment which pushes a people to live in the interior of its territorial frontiers, a sentiment which has created this network of nations. If I had discovered the *Algerian nation*, I would be a nationalist and I would not blush from it as from a crime. Men who have died for the patriotic idea are daily honoured and respected. My life is not worth more than theirs. However, I would not die for the *Algerian Fatherland*, because this Fatherland does not exist. I have not discovered it. I have interrogated history, I have interrogated the living and the dead; I have visited the cemeteries; no one has spoken to me of it. . . . One does not build upon the wind. We have dispelled once and for all the mists and the phantoms to link definitively our future to that of the French achievement in this country. . . . No one, moreover, seriously believes in our nationalism. What one wishes to fight behind this word is our political and economic emancipation. . . . Without emancipation of the native, there is no durable French Algeria. . . .

The various personalities which made up the Federation all favoured the assimilationist Blum-Violette proposal, and were greatly encouraged by the 1936 victory of the Popular Front Government in France. The possible failure of the proposal led to strong reactions on the part of Dr. Bendjelloul and his political associates. In 1937, he strongly attacked the French administration and called for the resignation of all Muslim elected representatives if the proposal was not voted upon. Some 3000 Muslims in the Constantine area abandoned their offices, but the response was small in other Departments. By January 1938 the Muslim representatives returned to their posts on the assurance that the Blum-Violette proposal would eventually be discussed. There is no doubt that the French Parliament's failure to take up the measure was a turning point in the thinking of many moderate Muslims. Ferhat Abbas had realized that the Muslims were too weak to oppose colonialists in Paris and Algiers, at the same time. He had enlisted the support of the Metropolitans in his demands for more equal treatment. And even the most liberal of them had disappointed him.

The Regnier Decree and other repressive measures along with the delay of the Popular Front in introducing reforms contributed to a short-lived unity of Algerians. In June 1936 representatives of the Westernized *élite* including Dr. Bendjelloul and Ferhat Abbas, Messali and his ENA followers and Communists sponsored a Muslim Congress in Algiers. The Congress voted a Charter of reformist demands.[8] But unity lasted only until 1937, when, in July, the Communists and the *Ulema* joined to expel the ENA from the Congress. Shortly thereafter, Ferhat Abbas and Dr. Bendjelloul also disagreed sharply: Abbas feared Bendjelloul was becoming too conciliatory with the French; and, of the two, Abbas was closer to the Algerian peasant, Bendjelloul to the Muslim 'aristocracy'. Dr. Bendjelloul created the *Franco-Muslim Algerian Rally*, which included elements of the *Ulema*, the PPA, labour unionists, veterans and the Socialist and Communist Parties. Ferhat Abbas refused to participate in this grouping and formed his own *Popular Algerian Union*, designed to unite the Algerian masses with their elected representatives. 'To win [the battle], a mass action is necessary', he wrote explaining the formation of the Union. 'The market-places, the Moorish cafés, the least of the villages must be our field of action . . . we want Algeria to preserve its own countenance, its language, its culture, its traditions.'⁹ The eve of the war, then, saw the moderate educated Algerians ready to demand greater freedom, if not complete independence, for Algeria – due not primarily to rebellious desire or the sense of Pan-Arab or Pan-Islamic solidarity which animated the PPA and the *Ulema*, but to the refusal of France, under strong *colon* pressure, to accept them as equals even when they had attained a high degree of French culture. The 'dream' of Franco-Muslim co-operation none the less remained with the generation formed between the Wars.

REFERENCES

1 Lacheraf, *Le Nationalisme Algérien* . . . , p. 249.

2 In the first section of the resolution, the ENA demanded: (1) immediate abolition of the Native Code and all exceptional measures; (2) amnesty for all political prisoners; (3) absolute freedom to travel in France and abroad; (4) freedom of the Press, of association, of assembly, and political and labour union rights; (5) replacement of the Financial Delegations by a National Algerian Parliament elected by universal suffrage; (6) abolition of the mixed communes and the military territories, and the substitution of municipal assemblies elected by universal local suffrage; (7) access to public office for all Algerians and equal treatment of all office holders; (8) compulsory education in Arabic, access to schooling at all levels, creation of new Arabic schools, and the printing of official documents in both Arabic and French; (9) respect for the Koranic teaching that no Muslim should fight another Muslim; (10) application of social and working laws to Algerians, rights to unemployment aid for Algerian families and family allowances; (11) expansion of agricultural credit for small Algerian peasants, more reasonable organization of irrigation projects, development of communication, and non-reimbursable aid for victims of famines. In the second section, the resolution called for total independence, the recall of French troops and the formation of a national army. A National Revolutionary Government would carry out the following measures: (1) establishment of a Constituent Assembly, to be elected by universal suffrage; (2) universal suffrage at all levels and eligibility of all Algerians for all assemblies; (3) the use of Arabic as the official language; (4) return of all properties to the Algerian State, including banks, mines, rails, ports and public services; (5) confiscation of large properties and the return of these lands to the peasants, respect for medium and small properties with the return to the Algerians of French State lands and forests; (6) compulsory free education at all levels in Arabic; (7) recognition by the Algerian State of the right of unions to form coalitions and to strike and to elaborate upon the social laws; and (8) immediate aid to the peasants by appropriations for agricultural credit bearing no interest for the purchase of machinery, seed and fertilizers, organization of irrigation and improvement of communications. The demands are contained in *L'Algérie Libre*, 11 March 1950, the organ of the *Movement for the Triumph of Democratic Liberties*, a successor to the ENA.

3 Lacheraf, *Le Nationalisme Algérien* . . . , p. 251.

4 The Salafiya adherents, seeking the causes of the decadence of Islam, denounced the heretical practices of the Muslim Brotherhoods, the saints, and other mystics, and asserted the supremacy of the Koran and the Souna (precepts taken from the conduct of the Prophet Mohammed). The Wahabists were even more strict in their attempts to purify Islam; and Sheik Abdo, a distinguished

professor at El Azhar University in Cairo, added the principle of modern science, believing that Islam admits of all modern progress. Politically, Abdo and his collaborators favoured the unity of Islam, although they also supported the pre-World War I Egyptian nationalist movement. Culturally they favoured a renovation of Arabic and a spiritual renaissance, again through the return to the pure principles of the past.

⁵ Quotations are cited in 'Les Ulémas Algériens Reformists', *La Nouvelle Revue Française d'Outre-Mer*, July-August 1955, pp. 328-37.

⁶ Julien, *L'Afrique du Nord en Marche*, pp. 109-10. Julien concludes that the negative content of the *The Young Algerian* is more significant than the positive.

⁷ The Federation sought increased representation for Muslims in all Algeria's elected assemblies; more equal treatment in the military services; the end of special courts for Muslims and greater participation of Muslims in the judicial process; reform of the forestry regulations including collective fines and other harsh penalties; extension of education; improvement of rural agricultural conditions; freedom of religion; improvement of workers' salaries and similar measures.

⁸ The Congress called for the end of all special Muslim laws; the re-attachment of Algeria to France; the maintenance of the personal status of Muslims; separation of the Muslim Cult from the State; the fusion of European and native teachings; freedom of teaching in Arabic and freedom of expression for the Arabic press; equal pay for equal work; assistance for the peasant; a single electoral college for all elections with universal suffrage and similar measures.

⁹ Cited in Julien, *L'Afrique du Nord en Marche*, p. 131.

Chapter 5

The War Period

T HE DEFEAT of France in 1940 was a blow to French prestige in Algeria. The collaboration of many of the *colons* with the pro-Nazi Vichy régime in France led to repressions against Algerian Muslims and Jews. The departure of both *colons* and Muslims to fight for France disrupted production, and several floods and droughts during the years between 1940 and 1945 added to the economic difficulties. The complete rupture of economic relations with France left Algeria with few industrial products and shortages of many basic items. While Nazi propaganda and quarrels between French generals and politicians diminished French standing still further in the eyes of Algerian Muslims, the Atlantic Charter and the growing strength of the Allies gave new impetus to Algerian aspirations for greater political liberty.

The pro-Vichy leaders in Algeria in 1940 and 1941 imprisoned most of the more radical nationalists. Messali Hadj liberated momentarily in April 1941, was sent immediately under house arrest to Reibell in the south of Algeria, where he remained until the war's end. Although many were in prison or in concentration camps, his followers continued their clandestine activities. Vichy's sudden withdrawal of French citizenship from Algerian Jews who had enjoyed it since 1870 and the Vichy Radio's praise for France's purely Christian greatness pushed Abbas and other moderates more and more toward Muslim nationalism. And General de Gaulle's appeals for resistance from London were not without their lessons for Algerians.

THE ALGERIAN MANIFESTO

The Allied landings in North Africa in November 1942 and the need for Free France to organize all available manpower to participate in the liberation gave Algerian Muslims new bargaining power. In December 1942 Ferhat Abbas and a number of other prominent Algerian elected representatives presented a series of demands to 'the responsible authorities'. This first 'message of representatives of the Muslims' was rejected outright by the French because it included American and other authorities in its appeal and because it made Muslim participation in the war effort conditional upon a Muslim conference.[1] Two days later, a somewhat altered text was presented to the 'French authorities', omitting any suggestion of an ultimatum. It stated that the Muslims, by their participation in the war effort, would assure their political deliverance 'in an essentially French framework'. It added that Muslim opinion was profoundly troubled and wished to be 'associated to the common lot other than by such sacrifices'. '. . . It is important to show it [Muslim opinion], by immediate and tangible achievements, the resolutely reformist will of France.' The signers then merely asked for the urgent calling of the proposed conference. As no satisfactory French reply was made, Algerian leaders went one step further and issued a formal statement of their grievances and demands.

The proclamation of the Manifesto of the Algerian People on 10 February 1943 was a cardinal step in the development of Algerian nationalism. Claiming to represent the views of 8 500 000 Muslims, the Manifesto was, in the words of Ferhat Abbas, 'a sincere and objective balance sheet of the past century' and a 'definitive and intended condemnation of an impossible assimilation. It asks for Algeria a veritable democratic and authentic national life.' In the words of the Manifesto itself, it is 'more than a plea, it is a testimony and an act of faith'. It did not deny French and Western culture, although it rejected the 'servitude' resulting from the French colonial system. The economic and social degradation under the French

occupation was such that Algerians felt themselves dis-
possessed and subjugated to the point of being foreigners in their
own country. Special attention was paid to the rôle of the *colon*
in preventing even the most Westernized Algerians from
achieving equality. The Manifesto concluded that European
and Algerian remained distinct, 'without a common soul'.
Referring to assimilation, the Manifesto declared: '*This policy
appears today, to the eyes of all, as an inexpressible reality, a dangerous
instrument placed in the service of colonization.*' Finally, it asserted:
'*The hour has passed when an Algerian Muslim will ask anything other
than to be a Muslim Algerian.*'

The Manifesto then demanded specific reforms, including the
condemnation and abolition of colonization, and the exploitation of the Algerian people by France. It called for the
application of the right of self-determination, and for a constitution for Algeria guaranteeing the absolute liberty and
equality of all inhabitants without distinction of race or creed.
The end of feudal property holdings by a land reform was also
sought, along with more familiar changes. The Manifesto ends
with the declaration that the Muslims could not wait until the
end of the war for needed reforms. The Algerian people, it
declared, 'accept all sacrifices. It is for the responsible authority
to grant its liberty.'

This document, bitter and sometimes revolutionary in tone,
was signed by Ferhat Abbas, Dr. Bendjelloul and other prominent Muslims of more conservative views. It represents the most
serious condemnation of the French régime in Algeria made up
to that date by moderate and Westernized intellectuals who
had previously hoped for full participation in French cultural
life. Unlike the message to the French authorities in December,
the Manifesto did not infer that the proposed Algerian constitution should exist within some French framework. Indeed,
relations between Algeria and France were left undefined.

The Manifesto was presented to the French authorities on
31 March, and later to the Allies. The French Governor
agreed to study it and created a Commission for the Study of
Muslim Economic and Social Affairs. He also requested more

concrete proposals for reform, which were presented to him by the Muslim members of the financial delegations in late May. The resultant document, called the *Additif*, was much more precise than the Manifesto itself, and made a distinction between those reforms which should be undertaken immediately and others which might await the end of the war. It was also far more explicit concerning the ultimate political organization envisaged for Algeria. The delegates asked for '... the guarantee of the integrity and unity of the Algerian territory and ... the recognition of the political autonomy of Algeria as a sovereign nation, with *"droit de regard"* [right to oversee] of France and military assistance of the allies in case of conflict'. They also noted: 'The formation of this Algerian state does not exclude ... the organization with Morocco and Tunisia of a Federation of North African states or a North African Union which appears to many minds as the best formula of the future.' The proposal for a constitution for the Algerian state could, however, be adjourned until the end of the hostilities and until the Algerian people could be consulted through a plebiscite.[2]

The *Additif* of the Manifesto is the first important document by Algerian moderates to speak of an Algerian sovereign nation and an Algerian state – words not contained in the Manifesto itself. Clear that Algeria would have a large degree of autonomy, its own Constituent Assembly, and its own constitution, the *Additif* gives to France only an undefined 'right to oversee', perhaps a type of benevolent trusteeship. In this sense, the *Additif*, very much a document of the future, proved to be an excellent rallying point and propaganda weapon even in recent years. Its reference to a North African federation also revived, from a different quarter, the idea orginally contained in the North African Star. Shortly after the *Additif* was sent to the French authorities, Algeria was taken over by de Gaulle and General Catroux was named Governor. Catroux rejected outright the demands of the moderates and asserted that France would never consent to the independence of Algeria.

The French refusal, for the second time, to accept the

Manifesto as a basis for discussion of reform led to strong Muslim reaction. In September, the Muslim delegates refused to partici-pate in an extraordinary session of the financial delegations, thereby demonstrating their loyalty to the Manifesto. Catroux responded by dissolving the Muslim section and by placing Ferhat Abbas and others under house arrest. Only after a delegation made an apology and declared its desire to have Algeria develop within the framework of French institutions did General Catroux revoke the dissolution. None the less, in December General de Gaulle, advised of the need of some constructive response to Muslim demands, made a speech in Constantine promising the reforms which later resulted in the March 1944 Ordinance. But measures which might have satis-fied the aspirations of the moderates in 1936, were now rejected by them, by the *Ulema*, and by Messali Hadj as well. Only a few moderates representing the financial delegations, who had disavowed the Manifesto under French pressure, received the new Ordinance with favour.

THE FRIENDS OF THE MANIFESTO AND OF LIBERTY

During the course of 1944, Ferhat Abbas successfully achieved on the organizational level the accord among impor-tant nationalist groups that the Manifesto had produced. In March, May and December 1944 he had conversations at Reibell with Messali and Sheik Ibrahimi of the *Ulema*. The exact content of these talks is not known, but in mid-March Ferhat Abbas founded the *Amis du Manifeste et de la Liberté* (AML) – the Friends of the Manifesto and of Liberty – with the aim of 'rendering familiar the idea of an Algerian nation and rendering desirable the constitution in Algeria of an autonomous Republic federated to a renewed, anti-colonial and anti-imperialist French Republic'. In social doctrine, the AML programme reflected the influence of the proletarian PPA. The programme proposed to 'make war on the privileges of the directing classes, to preach equality of men and the right to well-being and to a national life of the Algerian people'. Another plank called for the ending of the 'manœuvres of reactionary forces and of French and Muslim feudals and all those who have any interest in the maintenance of the colonial order'.

In September 1944 the AML published its weekly journal, *Equality*, for the first time with considerable success. During 1944 and 1945, the Central Committee of the AML claimed to have received more than 500 000 membership applications. But the unity of the AML, which for a second time brought together intellectuals and proletarians, modernists and traditional Islamists, was short lived. At its first Congress in March 1945, a conflict arose between the supporters of Messali and Ferhat Abbas. The newly admitted members of the PPA wanted to hail Messali as the 'incontestable leader of the Algerian people' and favoured an Algerian parliament and government. Ferhat Abbas and other moderates strongly favoured an autonomous Algerian Republic federated to France, as had the original programme of the AML. The PPA won this doctrinal battle by a large majority, thus accentuating the more radical content of the AML programme.

The radical turn of the AML and its large number of members led to repressive measures by the administration and made the *colons* more fearful and suspicious of the changes which de Gaulle had brought to Algeria. The first few months of 1945 were tense and explosive. In September 1944, Yves Chataigneau was appointed Governor-General and instituted a liberal policy. In March 1945, at the time that Messali's followers were impressing their views upon the AML, Arabs at the Congress of Heliopolis were discussing the formation of an Arab League, an event which had profound repercussions in North Africa. The deteriorating economic situation also added to *colon-*Algerian tensions. Algeria had been cut off from France during the War and in 1945 normal trade relations had not been fully re-established.

THE REVOLT OF 1945

The revolt which occurred in Algeria on V E Day, 1945, did not come without some warning. In late April, six European

General Councillors wrote a letter to the Prefect of Constantine demanding that 'instantly' measures be taken 'which, without provocation, alone will be of a nature to re-establish order and confidence in the French territory situated to the South of the Mediterranean'. The same month Messali was transferred from house arrest in the south of Algeria to Brazzaville, deep in Central Africa, to avoid disturbances. The administration found it necessary to 'adjust' the municipal elections for fear that certain radicals might be elected. In May, Ferhat Abbas appealed for calm in an editorial in *Equality*. Governor-General Chataigneau sent a circular to administrators throughout Algeria alluding to the possibility of troubles in connection with the victory celebration. On 1 May nationalist parades had occurred in several cities throughout Algeria, but without incident.

On 8 May, in Sétif, Algerians paraded in the streets to celebrate the Allied victory.[3] The local police tried to seize the banners carried by the crowd, an action which had not been taken in the course of other demonstrations. Shots were fired, and the crowd was dispersed; although it later reformed and attacked the police with rocks. The police again fired. The disturbances spread to other parts of Algeria, especially the heavily populated areas of the Constantine Department. In some places, dreadful atrocities were committed. The total casualty figures for the European population amounted to about 100.

The revolt was followed by one of the severest and most brutal repressions in Algerian history. The French Air Force, then under the direction of French Communist Minister for Air, Tillon, bombed and strafed many Algerian villages. French cruisers shelled the Algerian coast. The extent of the repression was kept from the Press. Official estimates, including those of the US officials on the scene, run from 17 000 to 45 000. The latter figure is the one claimed by Messali and most Algerian nationalists. The Governor-General's Commission of Inquiry into the revolt was cut short. In its report, admittedly incomplete, it cited a number of causes: the defeat and weakness of

France; Allied strength; Axis propaganda; the comparison made by Muslim soldiers of the Europe they had seen during the war with their low status in Algeria; enthusiasm engendered by the San Francisco Conference and 'misinterpretations' of the Atlantic Charter; inspiration of the Arab League and even of France's allies; and the many indignities suffered by Algerians. Besides the military repression, many nationalists and labour union leaders were imprisoned. Ferhat Abbas was arrested on his way to confer with Government-General officials, and the A M L was dissolved. Some of the more sensational trials included many PPA militants who were later to participate in the uprising of 1954. The repression carried out by the administration did little to prevent private acts of vengeance by *colon* vigilantes. The fact that local police have rarely given Muslims protection against these groups, which crop up whenever *colon*-Muslim relations are strained, has been a cause for lasting bitterness among Muslims.

The revolt of 1945 marked a turning point in Algerian history, both for the *colons* and for the Muslims. For the *colons* it was the height of the barbarism they had always attributed to the Muslims, as well as a shocking and a terrifying experience. At the same time, it was the beginning of a decline in their power, for in France not all shared the *colon* view that 'keeping the Muslim down' was the best answer. Between 1945 and 1947, Governor-General Chataigneau carried out liberal policies and created some hope that France might after all be willing to let educated Muslims participate more fully in their own affairs. After 1947, however, the *colons*, although defeated on the language of the new Algerian Statute, succeeded once again in sabotaging its liberal provisions.

For the Algerians who participated in the revolt, May 1945 was both a venting of long-pent-up frustration, and an indication of their own weakness *vis-à-vis* the *colons* and France itself. It is possible, but highly improbable, that the contention of the *colons* that the revolt was planned by Ferhat Abbas, Messali and Sheik Ibrahimi during their 1945 conversations is correct. It is also possible, and more probable, that the view of Algerian nationalists, that the revolt was a spontaneous response to *colon* provocation, is correct. In any case, the nature of the revolt indicates little planning or organization. Although the green and white flag of Algerian nationalism was on the scene, much of the violence seemed to have resulted from the more basic antagonisms which opposed poor and often hungry Algerians to more privileged and prosperous French *colons*. The repression which followed the revolt put many nationalists in prison, and they had ample time to meditate on the question of armed uprising against France. Some moderates were considerably awed by the French show of force and were led to accept the necessity of some kind of a compromise with France. Others concluded that the real task of Algerian nationalism was to make itself strong for a second test of force. Differing views of the events of 1945 led to the collapse of the unity achieved among nationalists around the Algerian Manifesto, and the AML was never revived.[4]

REFERENCES

[1] The full message to the 'responsible authorities' stated: 'If this War were, as the President of the United States has declared, a war of liberation of peoples and of individuals, without distinction of race and of religion, the Algerian Muslims would associate themselves with all their strength and by all sacrifices with this liberating struggle.

'They would thus assure their own political deliverance at the same time as the liberation of Metropolitan France.

'But it is fitting to recall that the populations which they represent are deprived of essential liberty and rights which the other inhabitants of this country enjoy, despite the sacrifices to which they have consented and the solemn and formal promises which have been made to them so many times.

'In consequence, they demand, before making the Muslim masses participate in any war effort, the convocation of a conference bringing together the elected and qualified representatives of all Muslim organizations.

'This conference will have as an objective the elaboration of a social, economic and political statute of Muslim Algerians.

'Only, in effect, a statute based on social justice is able to give to the Muslims of this country full consciousness of their present duty.'

[2] The election of a Constituent Assembly of Algeria by universal suffrage charged with drawing up the constitution and other provisions was spelled out in Title I of the *Additif*. Title II contained 'necessary and possible' reforms which could be undertaken immediately. The effective participation of Algerians in the government and administration of Algeria through the transformation of the Government-General into a government of Algeria with Ministers divided equally between Arabs and Europeans was the first of these reforms. The Governor-General would thus become the French Ambassador or French High Commissioner in Algeria. Algerians would have equal representation with Frenchmen in all elected assemblies, deliberative bodies and other organizations. The Delegates also required the immediate autonomy of administration of Muslim

villages in the mixed communes, with requisite changes of the local Councils and their Presidents into Municipal Councils and Mayors; immediate access of Muslims to all public functions, in equal numbers with the Europeans and under the same working conditions; the abrogation of all exceptional laws and measures and the application of common law within the framework of Algerian legislation. A second group of immediately desired reforms concerned 'equality before the tax of blood'. In the economic and social fields the Delegates demanded: the creation of an Office of the Native Peasantry; the creation of a Ministry of Work to apply laws to Algerian workers; the end of special native schools and the education of the many Muslim children not in school, along with the freedom of teaching in Arabic; development of Muslim villages; the abolition of the French shipping monopoly; and the end of the 'régime of directed economy', a régime prejudicial to Muslim products, traders and consumers; freedom of Islam; freedom of the press in both French and Arabic; abrogation of road and rail co-ordination laws; and the authority to establish three Muslim newspapers in Algiers, Oran and Constantine.

³ For the facts concerning the revolt, I have relied extensively upon an unpublished monograph by Manfred Halpren, entitled *The French in Algeria: 1944-1947.*

⁴ In its 5 May 1958 issue, *El Moudjahid* (The Freedom Fighter), official organ of the F L N, devotes an entire page to the revolt of 1945. The article favours the provocation thesis; is more detailed on French repressive measures than Muslim acts of violence. It cites as the death toll: 88 Europeans, of whom some were killed directly by or at the instigation of Europeans; about 45 000 Algerians; and 5,000 imprisoned, along with hundreds of burned villages. Noting that 8 May 1945 is an historic date, the article concludes: '. . . that day, the Algerian people lost its illusions and understood that it would never be free and respected until it was strong. . . . The Revolution began. . . .'

Chapter 6

Post-war Algerian Political Parties

THE ELECTION of October 1945 provided the first link in the post-war era between France and Algeria. The 1944 reforms were first applied in these elections for the first Constituent Assembly to draw up a French Constitution. The appeals of nationalists led to abstentions in the second college amounting to 50% in the Algiers and Constantine Departments, and about 35% in Oran. Of the thirteen seats to be chosen by the second college, the *Federation of Elected Muslims*, headed by Dr. Bendjelloul, obtained seven. The Constituent Assembly rejected the assimilationist proposals of Bendjelloul, and its consideration of Algeria centred on the question of an amnesty, finally voted, for those who had participated in the revolt of 1945.[1]

THE DEMOCRATIC UNION OF THE ALGERIAN MANIFESTO

Shortly after gaining his freedom, Ferhat Abbas formed the *Union Démocratique du Manifeste Algérien* (UDMA) – the Democratic Union of the Algerian Manifesto – at Sétif. The UDMA, unlike the AML, did not have a wide nationalist base but proposed to uphold the original programme of the Manifesto. On 1 May 1946 Ferhat Abbas made his well-known 'Appeal to Muslim and French Algerian Youth'. It was not only a profession of his moderate faith, but also showed the profound effect which the revolt of 1945 had had upon his thinking. Recalling his long career of co-operation with France, he asserted: 'If one thought, above all, has dominated my public life, it is certainly that of preaching – and of realizing –

ranco-Muslim collaboration, of favouring the culture and the
modern technology which form the indispensable cement of
.' He added: 'Union in democracy, fraternity in justice, have
een – and remain – my only political religion.' He criticized
he administration for its reactionary response to Muslim
fforts to achieve the desired co-operation. He accused the
dministration of provocation of the 1945 revolt, organization
f militia, and crimes and terror against the Muslim population.
Ie called for:

> *Neither assimilation, nor a new master, nor separatism.* A
> young people undertaking its social and democratic edu-
> cation, realizing its scientific and industrial development,
> carrying out its moral and intellectual renewal, associated
> with a great liberal nation; a young democracy in birth
> guided by the great French democracy: such is the image
> and the clearest expression of our movement for Algerian
> renovation.

urning to the critical point of his appeal, Abbas warned:
If Algerian youth does not dominate its differences of origin . . .
. will end inevitably in a moral suicide heavy with conse-
uences.' He ended: 'If all the Europeans of Algeria do not rid
hemselves of the colonial complex, of that pride of the con-
ueror . . . no Algerian community will be possible.'

The new party decided to participate in the elections for the
econd French Constituent Assembly. The success of its electoral
ampaign was overwhelming. The UDMA obtained eleven out of
he thirteen seats in the second college with about 71% of the
otes. This election marked the height of UDMA power in
Algeria; while groups favouring assimilation seemed to have
ost favour with the electorate. Following the election, Abbas
made clear his position concerning the immediate future of
Algeria. He continued to condemn assimilation and empha-
ized the permanence and originality of Algeria's personality.
Ie did not favour a Muslim state, but an Algerian state in
vhich Europeans and Algerians would have equal rights, in-
luding eventual universal suffrage and a single electoral

college. In August 1946 Abbas proposed an Algerian Constitu
tion to the Constituent Assembly, which was not, however
considered.[2]

THE ALGERIAN COMMUNIST PARTY

In all the election campaigns of the post-war era in Algeria
the European parties resembled in large degree those in France
In the second college, the Socialist and Communist Partie
tried to compete with the purely Algerian parties for Muslin
votes. The Socialists often attracted Muslim intellectuals, and
it was a Socialist Governor-General who from 1945 to 194[8]
raised such hopes for fruitful collaboration between Muslim
and Europeans. However, only the Algerian Communist Party
ever achieved substantial Muslim membership.

The Communist Party was established in Algeria in 1924 and
for fifteen years remained a branch of the French Communis
Party. At the Villeurbanne Congress in France in 1935, th
Algerian group obtained the right to form an autonomou
party, although in fact it continued to receive Moscow direc
tives through France. From 1935 onwards the Algeria
Communist line underwent many changes and contradictions
In 1936, the Party supported the demands of the Charte
drawn up by the Muslim Congress and the Blum-Violett
proposals. In 1938, French Communist leader Maurice Thore
at the Seventh Congress of the French Communist Part
declared: 'There can be no safety for the colonial people outsid
of the indispensable union with French democracy.' This stand
reflected the Party's participation in the French Popular Fron
Government. From its anti-Nazi position of 1938, the Algeria
Communist Party, along with many others throughout th
world, changed with the signing of the Nazi-Soviet Pact to a
'anti-imperialist' position. In 1939, the Algerian Communis
Party was outlawed at the same time Messali's PPA wa
dissolved, and it operated underground during the War.

In 1944 the Communists imprisoned or in concentratio
camps in Algeria were released and took up the threads c
political life once again. In France, the Communists were a

the height of their post-war prestige and power, due to their rôle in the French Resistance. The French Communist Party was in fact still primarily concerned with the war against Nazism. In June 1944, in *Liberty*, the weekly organ of the Algerian Communist Party, Etienne Fajon, European member of the Politbureau, wrote:

> With the aim of weakening the aid of the French people at a crucial moment, the enemy [Hitler] is reinforcing its radio campaign in Arabic to call upon the Muslim population in North Africa to separate from France. The agents of the enemy are carrying out here the same task of separation at the same time that they stir up the hatreds of the Europeans against the Muslims. It is not the Muslim populations who are calling for autonomy but rather the grand feudals, the multi-millionaires, the men of the trusts.

It was a Communist Minister for Air who ordered the bombing which followed the disturbances of 8 May 1945. On 12 May, in an appeal of the Central Committee of the French Communist Party for North Africa, Messali and other PPA chiefs and 'spies' were blamed for the revolt. About a month later, the Delegate of the Algerian Party to the Tenth Congress of the French Communist Party stated: 'Those who demand independence for Algeria are the agents conscious or unconscious of another imperialism . . . the Algerian Communist Party is struggling for the reinforcement of the Union of the Algerian people with the people of France.' At the same Congress, the Chief of the Colonial Section of the French Party asserted: 'It is necessary to denounce the plot of those who wish to divide the Muslims and to throw suspicion between Muslims and democratic France.'

The Algerian Communist Party favoured French sovereignty and assimilation in the early post-war period because Soviet Communism hoped to take over France with her colonies intact. But the elections of 1945 and 1946 in Algeria revealed that the Muslim masses would not vote for assimilationists. If the Communists were to obtain a Muslim following, then, some

D

modification in the line was called for. Such a change took place in late 1946. The vagaries of the Communist line and the opportunistic nature of the Party's policies were obvious to Algerian nationalists. None the less when they became victims of repressive measures of the administration, and when they saw that some short-term benefit for nationalism might be gained by a temporary alliance, both the followers of Ferhat Abbas and of Messali did not hesitate to utilize the Algerian Communist Party. The Party supplemented its influence over intellectuals through the French Communist Party's control of French labour unions. Algerian workers were forced to join branches of the French unions because there were no local Muslim unions at the time.[3]

The Movement for the Triumph of Democratic Liberties

Messali Hadj and his followers re-entered the political fray for the first elections under the Fourth Republic. Liberated by the official end of the war, but still prevented from entering Algeria's large cities, Messali returned from exile to Bouzareah, near Algiers, in October 1946. Surrounded by his associates, Dr. Lamine-Debaghine, Hussein Lahouel, Ahmed Mezerna and Mohamed Khider, he founded the *Mouvement pour la Triomphe des Libertés Démocratiques* (MTLD) – the Movement for the Triumph of Democratic Liberties. The MTLD, which replaced the still illegal PPA, favoured an Algerian Constituent Assembly, sovereign and elected by universal suffrage without distinction of any kind; the evacuation of Algeria by French troops; return of expropriated lands; Arabization of secondary education; and return of the mosques to purely religious control. Messali decided to participate in the November elections to put this programme before the Algerian people and to test the idea of Algerian independence at the ballot box. He therefore rejected efforts of the Algerian Communist Party, now hard pressed in the first college, to participate in a United Front, to include the Communists, the MTLD, the UDMA and the *Ulema*. Ferhat Abbas and the UDMA regretted Messali's stand, but decided not to participate in the electoral campaign to avoid a division among nationalists and permit Messali a chance where he had failed.

The results of the election in the second college were disappointing to the MTLD. It obtained five seats, including the election of Mezerna and Khider from Algiers and Lamine from Constantine, out of the total of fifteen. But it received only 153 153 votes out of a total of 464 319 who voted and 1 245 108 who were eligible. Eight seats in the second college went to administration-supported independents favouring 'Franco-Muslim co-operation', and two to the Communists. In the elections for the French Council of the Republic, the outcome was somewhat different. Despite efforts of the administration to exclude the UDMA in the indirect election, it ultimately received four out of seven seats, with three going to independents who favoured 'Franco-Muslim co-operation'. This success showed that the UDMA had retained the popularity it had achieved earlier, even though it had taken no part in the elections for the National Assembly.

The French National Assembly had before it four proposals for a Statute for Algeria, presented by the Government, the Socialist Party, the Communist Party and the UDMA joined by the Independent Muslim Group for the Defence of Algerian Federalism (the name selected by those Muslims favouring 'Franco-Muslim co-operation'). In the Assembly, the views of Algerian nationalists were presented by MTLD deputies. On 20 August, a date which the MTLD called 'historic', four MTLD deputies argued fervently that Algeria was not French; that it did not recognize the *de facto* situation created by the French conquest of 1830; that Algeria would not recognize any Statute unless it implied the return of sovereignty to the people. They called for a sovereign Algerian Constituent Assembly to be elected by universal suffrage without distinction of any kind, the proposal often reiterated by the MTLD in postwar years.[4]

In the Council of the Republic, it was the UDMA which put forth the Algerian views in the form of a proposal for a statute. 'It is the Europeans of Algeria who, for seventy-five years dictated its Muslim policy to the Metropole', said a UDMA delegate. There had been many policy changes: collaboration, assimilation, association, autonomy, reattachment, but none had been realized. 'The only policy really practised in Algeria is that called "French preponderance".' The proposed statute provided for full autonomy for Algeria and the recognition of an Algerian Republic with its own parliament and government, in a federalist relation with France. Other articles provided dual citizenship for Frenchmen and Algerians in both France and Algeria; two official languages with compulsory education in both French and Arabic; and agrarian reform. The Algerian Republic could form a North African federation with Tunisia and Morocco within the French Union. The UDMA proposal in the Council, as the MTLD presentation in the National Assembly, was not considered seriously by the Government. The experience of the two parties in the first elected parliament was therefore no more fruitful than that of Algerian representatives in the first and second Constituent Assemblies.

On 21 August the committee of the French National Assembly considering the Statute accepted the compromise version presented by the Government. MTLD members left the chamber and refused to take part in any further debate. On the 27th the Statute was accepted by the Assembly as a whole. In the Council of the Republic, the UDMA delegates abandoned their seats, after expressing their disappointment. UDMA leader Mostefai declared that the party could not accept the Statute adopted by the Assembly:

> This Statute is not assimilationist while seeking to be so. It is not federalist, as much as that is needed. It has nothing democratic in it although born in the sadness and wounds of the Grand Liberation. It is not progressive, since it takes away with one hand that which it gave with the other. It is a Statute without personality, without originality, without breath and without soul. Its only originality, if it is one, is to have maintained, under a new form, the ancient privileges of the lords of the land. It

substitutes only a golden chain for the iron chain which already bound us.

REFERENCES

[1] The principal work of the Assembly, the first Constitution for the Fourth French Republic, was rejected by the French people in a subsequent referendum.

[2] The UDMA proposal would have made Algeria an autonomous republic with its own government and flag, independent within the framework of the French Union. Algeria would also have had its own parliament, elected by universal suffrage, with legislative power and executive power in the hands of a President of the Algerian Republic, assisted by a Council of Ministers. France would have been represented in Algeria by a General Delegate acceptable to Algeria with consultative status.

[3] Quotations in the above paragraphs were taken from Darius Le Corre, 'De "l'Indépendance" de la Bretagne a "l'Indépendance" de l'Algérie', *Le Populaire de Paris*, 10 October 1957.

[4] Ahmed Mezerna outlined the economic injustices suffered by Algeria during the period of French occupation:

> 'It suffices to walk along the Rue de la Lyre in the evening, in Algiers, where hundreds of poor wanderers sleep on the sidewalk, or to examine the bands of men, women and children and aged, almost totally naked, whom misery and fear of death has pushed toward the cities and who, each morning, search the garbage pails, disputing with dogs and cats the remnants of food, the rags and the empty tin cans, to get an idea of the unbelievable human drama which is going on in Algeria.'

Chapter 7

Algeria under the Statute of 1947

D ESPITE the dreadful events of 1945 and the disappointments of 1946 and 1947, the Statute of 1947 might have provided a flexible framework for the political development of Algeria's Muslims, had not the years between 1947 and 1954 seen a rise in *colon* power. During this period, Metropolitan France was preoccupied with the long and unsuccessful war in Indo China, troubles in Tunisia and Morocco, political struggles and economic difficulties at home and the events of the Cold War. In Algeria itself, the *colons* proceeded to sabotage the new Statute. They pointed, for example, to the almost complete MTLD success in the municipal elections of October 1947, to the MTLD slogan, 'the suitcase or the coffin', and to the general extremist tendencies of the Muslim population in early 1948. They forced the resignation of liberal Governor-General Chataigneau, who was replaced by Socialist Marcel-Edmond Naegelen, who like one of his more recent successors, Lacoste, was a leftist in France, but a rightist in Algeria.

Naegelen took vigorous measures to limit nationalist activity and to prevent its expression within elected assemblies. To assure the supremacy of 'French presence' in Algeria he resorted to extensive rigging of the elections for the first Algerian Assembly in 1948 and its renewal in 1951, as well as lesser local elections. In the April 1948 election, the MTLD received only nine of the sixty seats in the second college; the UDMA received eight; the remaining forty-three seats went to candidates favouring 'Franco-Muslim co-operation'. In the partial renewal of seats for the Assembly, which occurred in

1951, the MTLD lost four of the nine seats it had held, and the UDMA lost one of its eight seats.

A dispute between the French Government and Governor-General Naegelen over election irregularities led to his resignation in 1951. His successor, M. Leonard, a former Prefect of Police, none the less continued to 'adjust' the elections. In those of June 1951 for the French National Assembly, the results were almost more than could have been desired. The MTLD lost all of the five seats it had held in the first Assembly, and the UDMA also lost all of its previous representatives. Among these, Ferhat Abbas failed to gain re-election in the town of Sétif, where he had founded the AML and the UDMA.

The effects upon the *colons* of these successes in sabotaging the 1947 Statute did not serve to increase *colon*-Muslim understanding. The fears so strong in 1947 abated, and the need for accommodation with the nationalists appeared to decline. On the long-term results of this period, an eminent French historian has said:

> It is thus that, little by little, the liberal work of Governor Chataigneau disintegrated: the municipal centres stagnated; the rural improvement sectors were altered . . .; the proposals for rural communes were abandoned; the resettlement of the peasants was considered achieved; housing benefited especially those who possessed a certain capital and sufficient revenues, not the mass of those without homes; the mixed communes subsisted; the separation of the Muslim cult and the State was not realized; the departmentalization of the Southern Territories was rearranged into a timid design . . .; the industrialization, brilliantly started in 1947-8, ran into difficulties; even the scholarization, which was effectively carried on, suffered from the penury of credits which were accorded to it, so much that the school population increased faster than the schools.[1]

Another unfortunate effect on the *colons'* mentality was the general reinforcement of their prejudices against Muslims. The rigging of the elections brought to the Algerian Assembly administration-supported *Beni-Oui-Oui* (Yes-men), for the most part men of low calibre, often illiterate, whose subservience did not help the *colons* to appreciate the increasing desires of the Muslim intellectuals and middle-class nationalists.

Some of the more liberal members of the European group began to show concern at the widening gap between *colon* and Muslim. This 'neo-colonialist' group, always small, but intellectually competent and frequently outspoken, was best personified by the young Mayor of Algiers, Jacques Chevallier. 'Let us consider today', he said, 'that it is safer to have around one *semi-rebels* rather than servants.'[2] Chevallier and like-minded members of the Algerian Assembly formed an Inter-group of Liberals 'to cement Franco-Muslim co-operation and to safeguard certain liberties'. But its activities made little change in the overall political picture, and its efforts to bridge the gap between the two populations were unsuccessful. Nor did investigations by Metropolitan Deputies serve to change Algerian election practices.

THE CRISIS OF THE MODERATES

Most serious reactions to election irregularities came from nationalists who suffered so consistently from these practices. At the opening session of the Algerian Assembly in April 1948 Ferhat Abbas rose to protest the voting procedures and the arrests of many candidates, including those of the MTLD. When the *colon*-dominated majority refused to permit him to speak, Abbas withdrew, followed by other UDMA members, and was later expelled. Many of the UDMA intellectuals were bitterly disillusioned. Said Ahmed Boumendjel, lawyer, prominent UDMA leader, now high in rebel circles:

> The French Republic has then cheated. She has duped us. . . . One day, one will wake up with a Muslim Algeria gone over to the Oriental bloc. One will then take the occasion to cry about the ingratitude and to strike, without anyone thinking then of looking for the reasons for such behaviour. Certainly, one will attempt to discover

palliatives to gain time, perhaps it will be too late? The more so that a choice dictated by despair can only be, inevitably, a choice against France.[3]

The inability of the UDMA to participate in Algerian political life through representation in the Algerian Assembly and its failure to bring any satisfaction of the legitimate demands of its members, created a serious crisis in party ranks. Favouring revolution by evolution, it could not easily seek other avenues than the parliamentary institutions to which it was itself devoted.

In 1951 the UDMA joined with the other opposition parties in an effort to gain strength through unity. The UDMA, the MTLD, the *Ulema* and the ACP formed the *Algerian Front for the Defence and Respect of Liberty*, whose main objectives were: the annulment of the results of the legislative elections of June 1951; respect for the freedom of the vote in the second college; respect for the fundamental liberties of conscience, opinion, Press and assembly; and opposition to repression in all its forms. Liberation of all political prisoners and separation of the Muslim cult from the State were also in its platform. The Front was short-lived, like other post-war efforts toward unity among Algerian nationalists, and the UDMA did not gain the hoped-for strength, or more honest elections. United in their opposition to colonialism, the parties in the Front had divergent views on a positive programme for Algeria. Queried in April 1949 concerning its attitude toward the Algerian Communist Party, the UDMA stated that, without denying its attachment to the French Communist Party, it 'is the only [party] to have attempted, on the intellectual, political and social level – to understand and to interpret the will of emancipation of the Algerian People. As such, it is, in this country, one of the active defenders of those liberties which colonial imperialism has still let exist.' The UDMA noted, however, its divergences with the Communists on foreign policy, the latter following Soviet policies, while the UDMA espoused neutralism between the two blocs.[4] The UDMA and the Communists also differed in composition and on the doctrinal question of the class struggle.

Furthermore, the UDMA noted, the Communists had not succeeded in convincing their European members that national
emancipation was needed for Algerian Muslims. None the less,
the UDMA found co-operation with the Communists on a
parliamentary level 'perfectly normal'. With the *Ulema*, the
UDMA felt a close mutuality of interests in 'permanent defence
of Muslim values' and 'defence of the Arabic language'. The
UDMA agreed with the MTLD on the necessity for a North
African union, but disagreed with it on how best to achieve
independence: Abbas was still an evolutionist; Messali, at
heart, for revolution.[5]

In the early 1950s, UDMA strength and enthusiasm waned.
At its Conference of *Cadres*, held in Algiers in April 1954,
Ferhat Abbas noted the active struggles of Tunisia and Morocco
against France, while Algeria was apparently calm. 'In truth
the popular discontent is profound. . . . And our tomorrows
are heavy with sinister omens.' He concluded that the Statute
of 1947 was a 'dead letter'. In all the elected assemblies, 'the
quasi-unanimity of the representation of Muslims is in the
hands of the French Administration'. He added, as if re-
examining his own thoughts: 'If Paris continues to refuse to be
the arbiter and to give its accord to the violations of the law,
would it not be legitimate for Algeria to use this ultimate recourse
[force]?' Commenting on the rôle of the UDMA, he asserted:

> We must avow it, the gigantic mystification and the
> cynical swindling of which Algeria has become the victim
> since the promulgation of the reforms, has almost made
> us disappear. It is certainly evident that a progressive
> party which has based its actions on the respect of legality
> and which militates in favour of *'revolution by the law'*, can no
> longer advance when the public authorities make arbitrary
> an institution of State. There is all the drama of our Party.

Abbas none the less affirmed: '. . . our conception of an
Algeria, elevated to the rank of Republic, serving as a meeting
ground between Islam and Christianity, with all it implies of
firm reciprocal will to live in common and to co-exist, is

perfectly viable and realizable'. For the UDMA, he outlined its continuing tasks: the satisfaction of the immediate demands and the defence of the vital interests of the labouring classes; contact with the Arabic-speaking masses and the inaccessible peasants; and convincing the Europeans, particularly the poorer *colons*, that they are victims of the wealthy feudals.

In the months remaining before the outbreak of the rebellion, Ferhat Abbas and the UDMA made several appeals to France for the end of the arbitrary régime in Algeria, for fraternal co-operation and for a conference in Paris where the conflicting interests in Algeria might confront each other in a peaceful forum. None was successful. In October, Abbas hinted that it might be a long time before an Algerian Republic came into existence. In the meantime, the UDMA might have to reorganize its structure. The party finances showed a large deficit. When the rebellion did break out, despite all these signs and portents, the UDMA was surprised.

The crisis of the UDMA moderates must be ascribed primarily to French colonial policies. France's neglect and intransigence inevitably polarized Algerian opinion, leaving little room for moderate nationalism to survive between the *Beni-Oui-Oui* and the revolutionaries. The UDMA's lack of contact with the peasant and worker masses, and its basic reliance upon intellectual and middle-class support also left the heart of the Algerian problem untouched. The moderates' failure to make greater efforts toward the achievement of unity along the lines of the AML was critical. And, too, the UDMA did not mobilize foreign public opinion to add to its own pressures upon France for reforms. None the less, the UDMA did much to develop political maturity in the Algerian *élite*. Its final fusion with the rebellion in 1956 rallied intellectuals and contributed greatly to the broadening of Algerian nationalism's social base.

THE SCHISM OF THE EXTREMISTS

The MTLD's reaction to the collapse of the Statute of 1947 and election rigging was more violent and more internally devisive than that of the UDMA. Shortly after the passage of the

Statute, a group of young PPA militants, who had worked underground during the War period, proceeded to form a para-military force, the *Organization Speciale* (os). From 1947 to 1950, the os collected arms, trained recruits, and planned a strategy for the eventual take-over of Algeria. While they received the blessing of Messali, the young leaders of the os, Ait Ahmed, Ben Bella, Khider, and others did not succeed in convincing the MTLD leader that the moment was ripe for attack. To finance os operations, a few young soldiers robbed the Oran post office in 1948, carrying off about one million dollars. But the secret army, better and better trained, was not used. Morale and discipline relaxed, and in Constantine, in 1950, an incident occurred revealing the existence of the os to the French authorities. French police unravelled the threads of the secret network, arresting hundreds of os members, including Ben Bella, but left the Kabyle organization untouched. The Kabyle set-up was thus intact at the outbreak of the rebellion. The Central Committee of the MTLD met shortly thereafter and provisionally dissolved the os. The Committee concluded that it was not a good idea to have an army in existence for a long waiting period. Only a general staff and technicians needed to be trained more than a few months in advance. The dissolution of the os, however, led to certain bitterness between Messali and its younger leaders who had worked so hard to set up the force. The os organizational achievements and arms caches were to prove invaluable after 1954.

During the 1947-54 period, the MTLD also underwent other crises. It was the object of extensive repressions in Haussonvillers in 1948, Sidi-Ali-Bounab in 1949, and others in the Aurès, Constantine and elsewhere. These measures took their toll of local party workers and forced constant reorganization of the leadership. MTLD election policy became a focal point of internal dispute. The MTLD ran its candidates at the same time as it continued to call for an independent Algeria and carried on clandestine activities. Some young militants considered any MTLD part in French legal assemblies as treason while others felt it was the only way to make short-term gains. Messali Hadj, now ageing, was often restricted by legal sanctions, and in 1952 he was finally removed from Algeria and placed under house arrest in France. His physical absence and his increasing mysticism following a trip to Mecca in 1951 widened the gap between him and the younger members of the MTLD Central Committee.

In April 1953 the MTLD was able to hold its second National Congress, the first since 1947. The debates of the Congress clearly showed deep differences within the ranks on doctrine and organization, as well as personality clashes. Greeting the delegates at the opening of the Congress, Ahmed Mezerna viewed the MTLD as passing from the phase of agitation to organization and education. He called on the party to rally 'new forces' internally and redouble its external efforts. In a letter to the Congress, Messali laid particular stress on the international situation. French colonialism on its deathbed was now supported by the United States, he wrote, and the Soviet Union could and had in the past made deals to the detriment of colonial peoples. The MTLD therefore must count primarily upon itself. Messali went on:

> To be a strong Party, well organized and well disciplined, to educate the Algerian people so that it may play a rôle in all circumstances, to prove the real existence of our Party in the interior as well as the exterior, to attract the attention of international opinion by our daily combativeness, to have a foreign policy seriously established, to know how to utilize all the trumps in the interior and exterior domains, to possess a good organization, a good Press and good representation in foreign countries, to harmonize all this activity, these are so many of the tasks absolutely indispensable to go forward in our struggle. . . . To direct it is to foresee, to direct it is also to choose; to direct, to choose, to have imagination, the spirit of initiative and of audacity, are many of the indispensable qualities for the leaders.

The Central Committee presented its General Report to the Congress analysing the defects and prospects of the party.

The previous Congress had resulted in three important decisions: MTLD participation in elections; 'struggle in all forms' against colonialism; and a search for unity of the Algerian people. On the positive side, MTLD candidates made the administration use force to defeat them; the party reached greater numbers in Algeria; and possibilities of union among all nationalists had been created. On the negative side, election campaigns had cost the MTLD dearly in fines and prison time, and there were some cases of indiscipline among representatives. Opposing colonialism had meant the extension of party activity, education of militants and formation of *cadres*.

The Central Committee divided six years' span into the 'offensive' period (1947-8), when the MTLD presented its programme for a sovereign Constituent Assembly; the 'defensive' period (March 1948–January 1950); and the period of 'recovery' (1950-3). During the defensive period the MTLD reorganized, and managed to survive two serious crises: Berberism and the Lamine Case. The Central Committee called Berberism a 'sectarian deviation, of a racist character and communistic', and warned it would remain 'a trump of colonialism as long as it remains standing'. Behind this obscure Marxist vocabulary there lay a problem of much deeper import: an ethnic division between Arabs and Berbers in Algeria which the French colonial régime exploited and which could be used by Algerians themselves for selfish ends. As noted earlier, the Arab invasions of the Maghreb did not completely Arabize the indigenous Berber population: in Tunisia, it is estimated that 1% of pure Berbers remain; in Algeria, 29%; in Morocco, where French 'divide and rule' policy was most pronounced, 45%. In Algeria, the largest concentration of pure Berbers is in the Kabylia, an area of high population density, relatively high intellectual level and a high rate of migration to other parts of Algeria and to Europe. It is not surprising, therefore, that bright young Kabyles often played a leading rôle in Algerian nationalist activities, though not to the exclusion of leaders from other areas. The 'crisis of Berberism', then, was probably misnamed: it was a conflict of views between young and active intellectuals, some of whom happened to be from the Kabylia, and the older leaders of the party, some of whom happened to be more Arabized. All parties are subject to such 'conflicts of generations' and the MTLD was no exception. The Lamine case was an early symptom of another difficulty which was to beset the MTLD more acutely in later years. As a result of a personal disagreement with Messali, brilliant Dr. Lamine, who became Foreign Minister in the Rebel Government, was excluded from the MTLD and virtually withdrew from political activities. On the foreign policy level, during this period, the MTLD officially took a position against the Atlantic Pact. The French Government had integrated Algeria into NATO in 1949.

During the period of recovery, the MTLD was better organized and widened its scope, despite the deportation of Messali. On the matter of union among Algerian nationalists, the Central Committee commented tersely: 'It took a form which did not respond to popular aspirations.' In short, the half-European Communists, the moderate UDMA and the conservative *Ulema* were too much for the MTLD to juggle in the same coalition.

The Central Committee then indulged in some frank self-criticism – typical of the Communist method which the MTLD made its model. On a more precise content of its aim of independence, the Committee asked:

> Do we have the intention to create a free Algeria for one person in particular, for an oligarchy in particular? An Algeria which would be free in name, but which, in reality, would only be an instrument thanks to which an individual or some oligarchy would raise itself to power.
>
> Such is not our objective. We wish to create a state 'BY THE PEOPLE AND FOR THE PEOPLE', where Algerians, without distinction of race or religion, will be free and equal. We mean a democratic State. Therefore, *our first principle is* DEMOCRACY.

Here there is a suggestion of the objections of some of the Central Committee members to Messali's increasing tendency to take personal power. Rejecting a monarchy as out of date, the Central Committee selected a Republic as a second principle. For its third, it proposed economic prosperity and social justice.[6] Finally, the Committee chose religious freedom, in conformity with Islamic tradition.

On the matter of inadequate doctrine, the Central Committee examined its idea of nationalism: a nationalism unlike national chauvinism, defensive, liberating, democratic, non-communist and non-materialist. The Committee placed the revolutionary MTLD in Algeria's political spectrum between the Communists, in theory revolutionary with regard to means and ends but whose ideological content differed from that of the MTLD, and the reformists, the UDMA and the *Ulema*. It noted that no real revolutionary could exist without constant touch with reality.

The revolutionary must therefore descend from the pedestal of his theory to root himself in concrete life, in order to draw upon it and to verify there his principles of action.

In order to develop fully, the MTLD must begin to 'think on a national scale', where it had in its propaganda phase thought only on the party scale.

Considering its defects of strategy, the Central Committee pointed out that the struggle must be divided into many phases with intermediate objectives to be successively attained.[7] In one sphere, the Committee noted that the party had not often addressed messages to the European minority and when it had done so it was only to state that the MTLD did not wish to cut the throats of the French, or to 'throw them into the sea'. The Committee suggested greater MTLD effort to make known its view that the French have a right to live in Algeria and that they will be considered Algerian with the same rights and duties as others. The party should also inform the minority about the repression practised against the Algerian people.

Finally, the Committee considered tactical deficiencies. The MTLD had been at times too intransigent in its policy of alliances with other groups; at others, too flexible. The Committee favoured the continuance of alliances with all parties willing to oppose colonialism, whether or not they shared the MTLD's ideas and methods. The party should also have an electoral policy, with carefully selected candidates; a detailed political programme, and propaganda adapted to all social levels. This part of the Report is particularly full of hints as to the nature of the Central Committee's opposition to Messali's policies. Its reference to the need for the revolutionary to descend from his pedestal is most probably directed at the MTLD's august Honorary President. The comments that some of the MTLD's doctrines and propaganda have lacked subtlety may be addressed to the less educated leader. Thinking on a party level, remaining too long in the stage of agitation and over-concentration on the political and verbal battle might also be ascribed to Messali by his younger, more impatient but more methodical lieutenants.

In a third section of the General Report, the Central Committee analysed Algeria's prospects for international help. It saw an important strategic rôle for North Africa both between the two world blocs and in the conflict between colonial powers and anti-colonialist Asia and Africa. France, 'intransigent' toward the aspirations of its colonies, would soon come into increasing conflict with the United States which 'constrained by the North African national movement and the Arab-Asian bloc, will act in a direction conforming to the aspirations of the Maghreb'. The MTLD policy of 'vigilant neutrality' remained valid for the foreseeable future, the Committee asserted. Commenting on 'the Conjunction of Internal and External Factors', the Committee noted the important support of the Arab-Asians in internationalizing the Tunisian and Moroccan questions and the vital need for both internal action and external support for Algeria's own fight. In their separate struggles, the three North African movements appeared out of harmony, but the Committee concluded it was not 'prudent' to hope for North African unity in the near future. The discussion of foreign policy seems to indicate general agreement with Messali's own neutralism, and to excuse in some measure the failure of the MTLD to support Tunisians and Moroccans more vigorously. In general, the Committee, with considerable insight, placed Algeria in a world context and showed greater interest in foreign affairs than UDMA leaders.[8]

The crux of the Committee's report concerned the party itself: the MTLD was a party of mass and not of opinion, like the UDMA. It concluded:

> For a party of mass, individualist tendencies and acts contrary to the discipline and the unity of the party cannot be tolerated. Militancy is required of all the constitutive elements of the party of mass. The party of mass envisages several methods of action. It accords a capital importance to the basis of its activity: ORGANIZATION.

The MTLD Congress passed a resolution responding in detail to the General Report of the Central Committee. It also addressed messages to the Algerian people on unity; to political prisoners; to Messali, assuring him of the party's unswerving attachment to the ideal which he represents: to the Moroccan and Tunisian peoples, calling for the reinforcement of Maghreb unity; to the Arab League, thanking it for its assistance to the North African cause; and, finally, to the Arab-Asian group, which, was 'called to play a rôle of the first order in the future of the world'.

In December 1953 *Free Algeria*, organ of the MTLD, launched an appeal for an Algerian National Congress signed by Hussein Lahouel, Benyoussef Benkhedda and Abderrahmane Kiouane on behalf of the Central Committee.[9] It called upon Algerian peasants, workers, traders, women, youth, students and intellectuals to unite. The Congress would represent all political parties, cultural, social and economic organizations, independent democratic persons and others. Its charter would have as its basis the national ideal. In February, Kiouane wrote in an editorial: the Algerian people has pronounced itself for the Congress. He explained that the MTLD called for abstentions in the Algerian Assembly elections because political conditions were not favourable to the formation of the Congress at that time. Later in the month, Lahouel told the Communists that the MTLD saluted its desire to participate in the Congress, but believed the idea must become better known to the masses before it could be held. He observed that the unsuccessful Front of 1951 was more an agreement of the parties than of the masses. Ibrahimi, leader of the *Ulema*, joined in the appeal for union.

Early in March, Lahouel wrote an editorial in *Free Algeria* discussing the lessons of seventeen years of struggle. At the second MTLD Congress in 1953, he asserted that the principle of collective leadership and of submission of the minority to the decisions of the majority had been affirmed. Collective leadership diminishes the chance of error – '*It expresses the fundamental spirit of our Party:* a spirit at the same time democratic and revolutionary.' The submission of the minority to the decisions of the majority was '*the expression of the great law of ideological and organic discipline:* discipline which creates cohesion and strength and permits organized action in time and space.' An examination of the 1953 resolution does not, indeed, reveal any specific reference to the principle of collective leadership. But Lahouel, who was soon to give his name to a faction of the MTLD, pointed out the main issue in the growing dispute between the Central Committee and Messali. If no one was to escape discipline, and discipline meant the acceptance by the minority of the majority's decisions, then Messali himself would have to accede to a resolution of the Central Committee with which he might be in personal disagreement.

Later in March, Kiouane editorialized: the Congress will respect the independence of the parties. Suggesting that the proposal had run into party objections, he admitted that it was then impossible to form a single party in Algeria due to colonialism and ideological pressures. But the Congress, 'union not unity', could be realized immediately. The Congress might develop into a party like India's Congress Party. Still later in the same month, Benkhedda wrote in *Free Algeria*: 'The idea of a Congress is becoming more popular every day.' This editorial appears to be the last mention of the question of a Congress and may therefore be the date at which a real break between Messali and his Central Committee occurred.

On 16 May *Free Algeria* saluted the fifty-sixth birthday of Messali with these words: 'The struggle of Messali and of the National Movement for Liberation of Algeria is identical.' Reviewing the life of the MTLD leader, it concluded: 'Whether MESSALI is at Niort [France], or in Algiers, he remains the symbol of our combat and the clairvoyant guide of the struggle for liberty.' In subsequent weeks, meetings and demonstrations by the MTLD occurred in Algiers and in France. At these gatherings only two Central Committee members, Ahmed Mezerna and Moulay Merbah, were prominent.

In early August, *Free Algeria* announced in banner headlines that an extraordinary congress of the MTLD had been held in mid-July in Hornu, Belgium. For about three months, the Party had gone through 'a terrible internal crisis' which had seriously affected its functioning. But it had been resolved at the congress with the 'unanimous condemnation' of certain members of the Central Committee for political deviation and serious errors. To its internal indecision and inaction, the Central Committee had added failures on the North African and international levels. It had not achieved real solidarity with Tunisia and Morocco; and internationally the problem of Algeria remained 'ignored'. At the congress, the MTLD reaffirmed its will to follow a 'sane, energetic and effective' political line, leading to the dignity and glory of the party. The congress expressed its total confidence in Messali to straighten out MTLD difficulties and unanimously elected him President for life. Some weeks later, after apparent unsuccessful efforts at reconciliation, the MTLD dissolved the Central Committee. From Niort, Messali announced the exclusion from the party of Benkhedda, Lahouel, Kiouane, Ben Badis, Ferroukhi, Yazid, Louanchi and Bouda for deviation, disobedience, misuse of funds and refusal to restore party property. Later on, *Free Algeria* said there had been no schism in the MTLD, but only regrettable tendencies, now corrected. Then it again turned its attention to French repression in Algeria.

The Lahouelist or Centralist faction of the MTLD held its own extraordinary congress in mid-August in Algiers. It rejected

Messali's accusation of deviation; confirmed the policy of the 1953 congress; removed from all their party functions Messali himself, Mezerna and Moulay Merbah; and denounced the Belgian 'fractional' congress. In the first issue of *The Algerian Nation*, the organ of the Centralists which appeared between September and November 1954, the new faction explained its view of the true origin of the MTLD crisis. The conflict began when Messali demanded full powers from the newly-formed Central Committee in September 1953. The Committee had admittedly excluded Mezerna and Moulay Merbah, close associates of Messali, from the leadership, but had barely begun the tasks set out for it by the second MTLD Congress. The Committee asked Messali to reconsider; then sent a commission to confer with him at Niort, which did not succeed. In January 1954 Messali renewed his demands, and this time threatened to withdraw his support from the Secretary-General and the whole Committee. 'The Central Committee believed, on the one hand, that personal power was inconceivable in a revolutionary party, and, on the other hand, that the situation did not permit the vesting of full powers in one man.' The Central Committee proposed a congress to decide the issue. A second commission sent to Niort to discuss this proposition was refused. The Central Committee then accused Messali, along with Mezerna, of undertaking efforts to play off party workers against the Central Committee through the formation of their own Committee of Public Safety and other tactics. In March, the Central Committee, not yet ready for an open break, conceded to Messali a part of the full powers he had demanded. Messali, Mezerna and Moulay Merbah then began to eliminate opposition within the party by 'coercive measures' and to prepare a congress which the Messalists would be certain in advance to dominate. The Central Committee refused to attend the Hornu congress and thereafter held its own in Algiers.

The Central Committee looked candidly at the real nature of its dispute with Messali. What Messali called reformism on their part was in fact the 'revolutionary realism' of the 1953 congress, asserted the Centralists:

To the policy of consolidation and enlargement of the forces of the Party, to the building of foundations indispensable to success and to the intensification of our struggle, to the work of formation and serious preparation, to the search for a solid union of all the sane forces of the nation, Messali wished to oppose verbal violence, agitation for agitation's sake, sectarianism and adventure.

In reality: 'The conflict had as its profound causes the questions of leadership and methods.' Messali wished to institute his personal power, while the Central Committee favoured collective leadership and 'democratization' of the party. Messali was 'against the theoretical work looking to the establishment of a precise doctrine which would permit the carrying out of the struggle on more and more scientific and rational bases, because he was afraid of being by-passed.' The Central Committee made this declaration of faith: 'THE STRUGGLE FOR THE GLORY OF THE COUNTRY AND NOT FOR THE GLORY OF A MAN.' The Central Committee also noted bitterly that while Messali was in his 'ivory tower' militants sacrificed themselves and built the party by their labours.

It is fundamental that the militants and the people know this and that there is brought to an end the absurd pretension of Messali to consider himself, alone, the equal and even the superior of the whole of the Party, indeed of the Algerian people. The belief in the indispensability of an individual must be ended. . . . The militants did not enter the Party because Messali is the President, but because it is the Revolutionary Algerian National Movement.

This nationalism, now to be favoured by the Centralists above the 'adventurism' of Messali, was founded neither upon race nor upon religion, but was essentially the 'will to struggle for the political, economic, social and cultural liberation of the Algerian people'. After the break, the Centralist faction again turned its attention with increasing urgency to the question of unity and the Algerian National Congress. They felt this unity essential to a more effective struggle against France.

The schism between Messali and the Central Committee of the MTLD was not merely one of personal power *versus* majority vote, the party *versus* the Algerian National Congress, propaganda and politics *versus* action in all fields. It was also a 'conflict of generations' and a quarrel brought about by the physical separation between Messali and the MTLD, a separation which had always worked to the detriment of continuity and growth of the party. Messali, the leader and founder of the MTLD, was ageing. He had grown up in an era when stirring speeches, mass demonstrations and the presentation of dramatic demands seemed almost all that could be accomplished by an embryonic national movement, fighting a powerful French colonial policy. The more youthful members of the Central Committee had been touched by their clandestine and anonymous lives, by the defeat of France in 1940, and by the apparently successful struggles of many countries in the postwar era to achieve independence, despite surprising odds. In any case, the split in the MTLD further fragmented Algerian nationalism and seemed to push even farther away the day of unified active opposition to France. When the rebellion broke out in Algeria on the night of 31 October 1954, Messali, the 'Father of Algerian Nationalism', was uninformed and, for the first time, really by-passed by events.

REFERENCES

[1] Julien, *L'Afrique du Nord en Marche*, p. 335.

[2] Cited in Julien, *L'Afrique du Nord en Marche*, p. 332. Chevallier resigned as Mayor of Algiers after the events of 13 May 1958. His book, *Nous, Algériens*, well expresses the liberal viewpoint. His housing projects – started with Muslim co-operation – have made Algiers an impressive city.

[3] Cited in Julien, *L'Afrique du Nord en Marche*, p. 334.

[4] UDMA neutralism, brought upon Algeria by its geography and position as a dependent country, was also based on fears of American liaison with colonial capitalists in Algeria, the Marxist belief that the United States would choose war rather than economic crisis, and Algeria's involuntary participation in NATO.

[5] The interview from which the above quotations were taken is cited in Jeanson, *L'Algérie Hors la Loi*, pp. 113-19.

[6] In the economic sphere, the Committee outlined the following objectives: creation of a truly national economy in place of the colonist one then existing; agrarian reform; industrialization; nationalization of the basic means of production; and harmonization of the Algerian, Moroccan and Tunisian economies in order to make a common market both of production and consumption. In the social field, the Central Committee proposed: an increase in the standard of living, equitable distribution of the national income, and freedom for trade unions. Culturally, the Committee proposed the spread of a national culture related to

Arab-Islamic culture, the spread of technical education, and a campaign against illiteracy.

[7] Several types of objectives are defined. The first, an objective-obstacle, is that of the struggle against the repression which must be immediate and continuous. Objectives of foundation, those which create para-political forces, include organization of the workers on the example of Tunisia; organization of youth; participation of Algerian women in the liberation; the building of a national culture, including a campaign against illiteracy and the spreading of Arabic. Objectives considered to be direct instruments of the struggle concern: party organization; organization of Algerian emigrants; the unity of the Algerian people; the spreading of knowledge about Algeria in foreign countries; and the development of national *cadres*. As a temporary objective, the Central Committee cites the policies of memoranda to the UN.

[8] The following more detailed description of the Committee's comments on the US and the USSR is considered valuable because of the prominence in the FLN, particularly in its foreign policy making, of some of the former members of the Central Committee. About Soviet policy in Asia and Africa, the Committee stated:

> It is fundamental to observe that the influence of Communism, while espousing the national causes and proceeding with the class struggle, stops *grosso modo*, in Asia, at the frontier of the Muslim countries.
>
> As far as the colonial countries are concerned, Soviet policy is in general favourable to their liberation. Such an attitude, which does not require any particular effort, is purely tactical; it is adopted with the evident aim of weakening the Occidentals. In fact, the supreme hope of this policy is to permit . . . a reinforcement of local communist parties. This tactic, which was able to succeed in Indochina, in Malaya and perhaps in India, did not succeed in a similar case in Muslim countries, notably in Indonesia and in Iran.

The Committee saw US policy as that of containing the political and ideological expansionism of the Soviets.

> 'The means of action chosen was first the economic recovery of Europe by the Marshall Plan, then Point IV, timid means which did not succeed in counteracting Communist influence. Then the military means was preferred to the economic. From then on, deterrent force became the principal means of action of the Americans.

The resultant policy of rearmament was 'shared if not imposed on their allies'. American aid resulted necessarily in the imposition of Washington's policies upon its allies. In sum, the Western bloc, however, presented many contradictions. Discussing the methods of the two blocs, the Central Committee stated: 'In the cold war, the Soviet bloc nearly always has the initiative. With its monolithic system, better organized on the propaganda level, leaning on a real force, benefiting from the open structures of the Occidental régimes, the Communists have from these facts truly led the game on the international chessboard.' The use of armed force is considered the essential method of the Western bloc, particularly of the United States.

[9] About 100 issues of *Free Algeria* were published between 1949 and its banning in November 1954. This weekly was the successor to earlier MTLD organs: *The Nation*, *The Algerian Parliament* and *The Algerian Nation*. Published first in Algiers, *Free Algeria* was seized and published thereafter in Paris. Numerous issues were subject to seizures and other repressive measures. In tone, *Free Algeria* was more violent and inflammatory than the UDMA's *The Algerian Republic* and contained more appeals and protests. Articles which appeared more than once over the year 1953-4 included a series on repression in Algeria; on the Algerian proletariat; on 'The Illustrious Men of the Maghreb'; Islam and Western ideology; news of the Arab League; and life among Algerian workers in France. *Free Algeria* placed considerable emphasis on Morocco, Tunisia, Egypt and other underdeveloped areas, giving little attention to France, Europe, the United States, South America, etc. After the split in the MTLD, *Free Algeria* appears to have represented the views of the Messalist wing of the MTLD only.

PART III

THE RESORT TO FORCE

The Algerian Front of National Liberation and Its Army

I N HIS classic description of the nature and development of revolution, Jules Monnerot states:

During revolution all the great forms and categories of social activity are progressively deprived of their autonomy; foreign war and civil war, foreign policy and domestic policy, economics and politics and religion – they all cease to be independent of each other. More and more everything 'hangs together', and this involves, both for individuals and groups, an ever-increasing stress and strain. . . . Finally, the whole world is no longer more than a vast sensitive area of friction and counter-friction. Interaction between microcosm and macrocosm, individual and society, substructure and superstructure, becomes dizzyingly swift, and men are swept along with it uncomprehending. . . . There is no longer a 'synthesis of values and aims' enabling each human group and each individual to 'find a place for everything'; and ethics breaks apart into incompatible duties; 'values in isolation make war upon one another', contending for the individual and within him. The historian can break the general crisis down into a series of particular crises at definite times and places; but the crises determine and modify one another, and their interdependence is both spatial and temporal. The ancient psyche is stirring to change, and as yet nothing has come to fill the void left by the things it has cast away. Needs are ill-formulated and satisfy themselves where and how they can. The *beliefs* on which society was founded no longer command organic assent, but are attacked and defended on grounds of interest; the great social impulses in the psyche which these beliefs represent are openly destroyed by criticism. . . .

In such a period, when the old basis of society is becoming undependable and fluid and is giving place to a state of transition, the criticism of everything upon which the old, and no longer satisfactory, state of affairs was based becomes unrestrained. . . . As a natural complement to the spread of scepticism, there is an outbreak of immature mysticism . . . 'the alliance of scepticism and nostalgia'. Side by side with nihilism (the state of psychological 'availability', which means that one is available for *anything*), there emerges in various forms a nostalgia for social consensus. In its longing for unity, the psyche will feed upon the grossest counterfeits of it: the golden age and the day of glory. . . . The new 'conceptions of the world', which attempt to fill the place of the old social order, have the fragility of newness. . . .

A revolution – the long crisis by which a multiplicity becomes a unity – can no longer take place within a 'sealed vessel', in one part of the world, not even in a whole continent. The interpendence of troubles is a universal interpendence. . . .

A revolution is an historical process which leads not to the gates of paradise but to a world similar to the one we know except that many of the things in it, including the psyche itself, have changed.

By what groups will goods and services be distributed and shared, and how will these groups be composed? For whom, or for whose profit, will things be distributed? What human relations will really be changed? And what will be the cultural significance of the change? What sort of new order will it be in which men will *accept* their status, and how will it establish the circulation of *élites*? These are the real questions, which reveal what is at stake in the battle.

. . . Broadly speaking, any age may be called revolutionary in which the increasing diffusion of troubles is approaching the saturation point. Dissension and divergence are reaching their maximum extension. . . . Society is no longer *accepted* by the majority, and an increasing number of men begin to lose their sense of 'belonging' either to the social order or to the world order. . . . Society becomes, to an ever greater extent and at last completely, an arbitrary arrangement or better, a succession of arrangements, which no longer deserve the name of 'society'.

The rôle of circumstance in making or marring a man's career seems to increase, while the rôle of responsibility diminishes; and in such times the great man is the one who, in addition to his other gifts, possesses the gift of discerning the 'favourable moment'. . . . To their other virtues the greatest men of such times seem to add an infallible knowledge and gift of social navigation. . . . When the individual no longer feels himself integrated within an order, he seeks provisional substitutes for it: the shelter of a faction or any safe situation. . . . But the situation appeals to the spirit of enterprise as well as caution. There are new opportunities, and with decision, courage, endurance, and luck much more may be achieved than during the preceding age.[1]

1954 was a revolutionary year for Algeria. Expressions of discontent and 'rising expectations' entered the electoral lists and were rigged to defeat; or they found their way to the Algerian Assembly and died there on the horns of *Beni-Oui-Ouiism* and *colon* predominance. Those nationalists who still cared to meet joined together to lament their growing impotence and dwindling funds, or to engage in hapless feuding. Nationalist confidence in any kind of peaceful development dimmed. Thoughts of force and violence increased. 'Dissension and divergence' were 'reaching their maximum extension'.

Below the fruitless debate, the great reservoir of the Algerian people – 5 000 000 close to starvation, the rest not very far from it – seemed outwardly calm. Ground more and more between its rising birth-rate and insufficient economic development, it waited, without active resistance. Its daily contact with the much richer, privileged *colons* served as an ever-present reminder of its inferior position; the treatment of Muslim victims of the Orléansville earthquake in the summer of 1954 underscored the racialist discrimination. The Algerian people, from peasants to professionals, were becoming 'available for *anything*'.

On the international scene, the leaders watched closely and the people heard rumours of the many new independent nations which had come into being since World War II despite heavy odds. Events in Tunisia during 1954 seemed to indicate that force, even of a few mountain fighters, might yield great results. In the West, the Moroccans continued to use terror to show their disapproval of the French deposition and exile of their Sultan. The whole Arab world seemed to be stirring.

The channelling of the deep Algerian currents of dispossession into a rebellion required, then, only leaders and arms. Messali's response to the disintegration had been to concentrate all powers in himself – perhaps the only man in which he felt trust. The Centralists had sought unity by first creating a new faction. There were others who possessed more of 'the spirit of enterprise' and who, unlike the moderates, were not limited in the means they could use to change the system. Their traditional leadership had failed them. They thought they discerned 'the favourable moment' to pass to the phase of direct action.

The Revolutionary Committee for Unity and Action

The *Comité Révolutionnaire Pour l'Unité et l'Action* (CRUA) – the Revolutionary Committee for Unity and Action – formed in early 1954, was founded by nine young men: Hussein Ait Ahmed, Ahmed Ben Bella, Mohamed Larbi Ben M'Hidi, Mohamed Boudiaf, Mostefa Ben Boulaid, Rabat Bitat, Mourad Didouche, Mohamed Khider, and Belkacem Krim.

Krim (Kabylie), Ben Boulaid (Aurès), Ben M'Hidi (Oran) Bitat (Algerois), and Didouche (North Constantine) headed their respective *Wilayas* (provinces), while Boudiaf, a skilful organizer, maintained liaison with the three others outside Algeria. Most of these young men were MTLD militants, came from the lower middle or lower classes of Algerian society, had had some experience in the French Army and the OS, and had been in French prisons. The founders of the CRUA blamed both the Messalists and the Centralists for the internal quarrels of the MTLD. They believed that party unity should be sought at the base rather than the higher echelons of leadership; each group of militants should break from both factions and freely discuss the crisis of the party. The CRUA, for itself, rejected the contentions of both Messali and his opposition. Politically, the CRUA leaned toward the Centralist view that unity was essential to success, but it differed on the necessary time-table. Unity was not required before seizing the initiative; on the contrary, action might be the best way to bring all patriotic Algerians together.

From March to October 1954, members of the CRUA held a series of clandestine meetings. Within Algeria, Krim and Ben Boulaid – representing the key Kabylie and Aurès *Wilayas* – met secretly in Algiers and agreed to take up arms against the colonial régime. They were later joined by the four other leaders and assigned responsibilities and objectives. At their historic meeting of 10 October, the fateful decision was taken to launch the revolt on All Saints' Day, 1 a.m. on the morning of 1 November. Meanwhile, CRUA leaders on the outside had met at 'vacation' spots in Switzerland, to organize arms purchases and obtain the support of other nationalists. A number of Centralists joined the movement, but all efforts to bring Messali and his closest lieutenants back into the fold proved fruitless.

On the night of 31 October–1 November, some thirty synchronized attacks were made throughout Algeria upon military and police targets. The attack was mounted by only 2–3000 militants, armed largely with hunting rifles and other local weapons. In most cases the small groups withdrew after their missions had been accomplished. In the Aurès, the members of the CRUA and their motley supporters – anyone who would take up arms – set up bases for continuing operations from mountain hideouts inaccessible to the French. The revolution – 'the long crisis by which a multiplicity becomes a unity' – had begun.

LEADERSHIP OF THE REBELLION

On the eve of the Rebellion, the CRUA was transformed into the Political *Front de Libération Nationale* (FLN) – Front of National Liberation – and the *Armée de Libération Nationale* (ALN) – the Army of National Liberation. A tract distributed in eastern Algeria on 1 November said only that the leaders of the FLN-ALN were 'a team of responsible and conscientious young militants'. The original nine of the CRUA were seconded by such men as Ouamrane, Abane and Nasser (Kabylie), Zirout and Ben Tobbal (North Constantine), Chihani and Nouaroua (Aurès), Boussouf (Oran) and Suidani, Dahlab and Benkhedda (Algiers). The leadership consisted primarily of military men, who possessed a great deal of power in making local decisions, and a few Algerians outside the country whose main function was that of obtaining arms and supplies for the rebels. The External Delegation, as it was called sometime later, was also important in setting up supply routes either through Tunisia or Morocco to be used in the opening of new military sectors. These young men ran the Algerian Rebellion until August 1956. During these months, they were joined by a number of other important individuals from the Central Committee of the MTLD, from the UDMA and *Ulema*, most of whom were added to the External Delegation, which gradually expanded its diplomatic activities.

The first meeting of the *Conseil National de la Révolution Algérienne* (CNRA) – the National Council of the Algerian Revolution – which took place in late August 1956 was many months in preparation. The idea of a national congress uniting leaders of all groups was one which had been previously suggested by members of the Central Committee of the MTLD,

and was taken up by a number of Army leaders, notably
Zirout of North Constantine. As a demonstration of their
military power, the military organizers chose the Soummam
Valley as the site – an area the French claimed to have
'pacified'. This choice of venue did, however, make arrangements for the conference and communication with external
leaders more difficult, and the meeting was somewhat delayed.
Assembled in the valley, the military leaders found themselves
cut off from the External Delegation awaiting news in Italy.
But the decision was taken, most probably by Abane, to hold
the congress in any case.

The CNRA set up by the Soummam conference was composed
of seventeen full members and seventeen associate members.
Among the full members were the original CRUA leaders still
living, new military leaders, Ferhat Abbas, who had gone to
Cairo in early 1956 to join the Front, Tewfik-El-Madani, leader
of the *Ulema*, and prominent MTLD leaders, Lamine-Debaghine
and Yazid. On the list of associate members were Ben Yahia,
who had organized the Algerian students for the FLN, Mehri,
a former member of the MTLD Central Committee, and Francis,
a leader of the UDMA and close associate of Ferhat Abbas, as
well as military men. The total membership of the CNRA was as
follows:

NATIONAL COUNCIL OF THE ALGERIAN REVOLUTION
20 AUGUST 1956
(unofficial)

Full Members

Hussein Ait Ahmed	Laksri Amara
Ferhat Abbas	Ben Aouda
Ramdane Abane	Lakhdar Ben Tobbal
Ahmed Ben Bella	Mohamed Ben Yahia
Mostefa Ben Boulaid	Boumediene
Benyoussef Benkhedda	Abdelhafid Boussouf
Mohamed Larbi Ben M'Hidi	Mahmoud Cherif
Rabat Bitat (in prison since	Slimane Dhiles
February 1955)	Ahmed Francis

E

Mohamed Boudiaf   Lamouri
Saad Dahlab   Ahmed Mahsas
Mohamed Khider   Abdelhamid Mehri
Belkacem Krim   Ali Mellah
Mohamed Lamine-Debaghine   Brahim Mezhoudi
Tewfik-El-Madani   Tayeb Thaalbi
M'Hammed Yazid
Youssef Zirout

The Soummam conference also elected a *Comité de Co-ordination et Execution* (CCE) – Committee of Co-ordination and Implementation – composed of five members whose names were kept secret. These were:

COMMITTEE OF CO-ORDINATION AND IMPLEMENTATION
20 AUGUST, 1956

> Ramdane Abane
> Ben Youssef Benkhedda
> Mohamed Larbi Ben M'Hidi
> Saad Dahlab
> Belkacem Krim

All were then leaders within Algeria itself. The CCE also reflected the primary importance of military action, as well as the virtual impossibility of dependable frequent communication between the internal and the external leaders.

According to the decisions of Soummam, the CNRA, 'highest organ of the Revolution, guides the policy' of the FLN and is the 'sole body authorized in the last resort to take decisions relative to the country's future'. ' . . . Only the CNRA is capable of ordering a cease-fire.' The CCE is:—

> a real war Council, and is responsible for guiding and directing all branches of the Revolution: military, political or diplomatic. It controls all the organized bodies of the Revolution (political, military, diplomatic, social and administrative). The political-military leaders responsible

for all Revolutionary activities in the six districts or Wilayas are directly responsible to the CCE.

The CCE set itself up in Algiers, although its members were often on the move. Committees, discussing various matters pertaining to present and future activities of the revolution, were to be appointed by the CCE to which they were made responsible.

The leadership of the FLN-ALN did not long remain what it had been in August 1956. Within less than a year, four prominent members of the External Delegation, Ait Ahmed, Ben Bella, Boudiaf and Khider, had been captured, and three members of the original CCE, Ben M'Hidi, Benkhedda and Dahlab had either been captured and executed or forced to flee Algeria to escape arrest. In late 1956, some members of the military leadership and those of the External Delegation met in Tunis and Cairo to discuss the results of the Soummam conference and to establish greater liaison between the two groups. Soon afterwards, the CCE moved its headquarters to Tunis, thus making the internal-external division among leaders less distinct.

In August 1957 the CNRA held its second conference in Cairo. There the membership was enlarged from thirty-four to fifty-four, with a view to establishing a forerunner of an Algerian parliament. The membership of the second CNRA was not made public, although it may be presumed that it included all previous living members of the CNRA who could still take an active part in the Revolution. All its twenty new members, to be named by the CCE, were not immediately appointed. The CCE was also enlarged from five to fourteen members, of whom five in prison in Paris or Algiers, were honorary members. A precedent for retaining imprisoned members on the CNRA had already been established and the leaders in Paris continued to be consulted by secret mail or occasional intermediaries. The Cairo conference left the functions of the CNRA and the CCE substantially the same. It was decided that the CNRA, 'sovereign organ of the Revolution', would hold an annual meeting.

To apply the policy defined by the CNRA, the CCE 'has extensive powers on all problems, except those which engage the future of the country, for example: negotiations, end of hostilities, alignment with one bloc or another, and international solution to the Algerian problem, intervention of a third party in the Franco-Algerian conflict, etc. . . .' The CCE was made responsible to the CNRA which could overthrow it by a vote of two-thirds. The full membership of the CCE was as follows:

COMMITTEE OF CO-ORDINATION AND IMPLEMENTATION
AUGUST 1957

Ramdane Abane
Ferhat Abbas
Lakhdar Ben Tobbal
Abdelhafid Boussouf
Mahmoud Cherif
Belkacem Krim
Mohamed Lamine-Debaghine
Abdelhamid Mehri
Amar Ouamrane

Honorary Members

Hussein Ait Ahmed
Ahmed Ben Bella
Rabat Bitat
Mohamed Boudiaf
Mohamed Khider

Unlike the earlier one, the CCE of August 1957 included external as well as internal leaders. Ferhat Abbas, former leader of the UDMA, was included along with former MTLD militants, Lamine-Debaghine and Mehri. These three became the principal architects of diplomatic policy on the CCE in the absence of the former External Delegation.

During the months which followed August 1957, the leadership of the FLN became increasingly involved in the establishment of common policies with its two independent neighbours,

Tunisia and Morocco. The Tangier meeting of the Moroccan *Istiqlal* and Tunisian *Neo-Destour* parties with the FLN, which took place in April 1958, provided for the eventual establishment of an Algerian government, following consultations with the Tunisian and Moroccan governments. It also called for the eventual establishment of a Maghrebian parliament, and a co-ordinating committee for the Maghreb. Consultations did not lead to the immediate establishment of the Algerian Government. But in June the CCE proceeded to designate specific governmental functions to its members. The functions were assigned as follows:

Information Affairs: Ferhat Abbas
Military Affairs: Belkacem Krim, Amar Ouamrane,
    Abdelhafid Boussouf
Diplomatic Affairs: Mohamed Lamine-Debaghine
Interior Affairs: Lakhdar Ben Tobbal
Financial Affairs: Mahmoud Cherif
Social Affairs: Abdelhamid Mehri

At last, the moment seemed propitious and on 19 September, 1958 the CNRA announced in Cairo, Rabat, and Tunis the formation of the Provisional Government of the Algerian Republic. On it were many well-known political and military leaders and some soldiers and organizers within Algeria, hitherto unknown to the outside world.

THE PROVISIONAL GOVERNMENT OF THE ALGERIAN
REPUBLIC 19 SEPTEMBER 1958

Prime Minister: Ferhat Abbas
1st Deputy Prime Minister: Ahmed Ben Bella
Minister of Defence and Deputy Prime Minister:
    Belkacem Krim
Minister of Foreign Affairs: Mohamed Lamine-
    Debaghine
Minister of Internal Affairs: Lakhdar Ben Tobbal
Minister of Armament and Supply: Mahmoud Cherif
Minister of Communications: Abdelhafid Boussouf

Minister of North African Affairs: Abdelhamid
   Mehri
Minister of Economy and Finance: Ahmed Francis
Minister of Information: M'Hammed Yazid
Minister of Social Affairs: Benyoussef Benkhedda
Minister of Cultural Affairs: Tewfik-El-Madani
Ministers of State: Hussein Ait Ahmed, Rabat Bitat,
   Mohamed Boudiaf, Mohamed Khider
Secretaries of State: Lamine-Khan, Omar Ouseddik,
   Mustafa Stambouli

The essential fact about the leadership of the Algerian
Revolution is not the absence of a single charismatic leader, but
the presence of leadership in depth. Lack of one top leader
may be explained by the attempts of Messali Hadj to dominate
the Algerian national movement – attempts bitterly resented
and resisted by other Algerian leaders, through fear that a
single leader might make disastrous decisions for personal
reasons, and by the necessity for continuity difficult for one
man to ensure in the dangers of a guerrilla war. This is not to
say that some at least of the political and military leaders have
not cherished the idea of becoming a single recognized chief.
And certainly a number of military men have wanted absolute
power on a small scale and some, indeed, seized it for a time.
But opposition by other leaders and devotion to the nationalist
cause have ended all serious attempts to usurp power. The
naming of former UDMA chief Ferhat Abbas as Prime Minister
in the Provisional Government has, for the present, obscured a
possible rivalry for leadership among the younger men who
made the Revolution. And Abbas will probably be the first
President of an Algerian Republic.

The obvious candidates for future leadership are Krim, who
will have Army and particularly Kabyle support, and Ben Bella,
a Vice-Premier despite his long imprisonment. Minister of
Defence Krim has for some time been the undisputed military
leader of the rebellion. Short, stocky and vigorous, he is both
loved and respected by the men with whom he has shared the

terrors and triumphs of the *maquis*. Krim was born in the Kabylia and raised on nationalist slogans. Like many other present military leaders, he did his tour in the French Army. In 1945 he was inspired by the ideal of unity of the Friends of the Manifesto and of Liberty and later by the boldness of Messali and the MTLD. He soon became an MTLD leader in the Kabylia and took to the *maquis* in 1947 to escape arrest. From his mountain hide-out, Krim led raids against the French and their Muslim collaborators and travelled secretly from village to village spreading revolutionary ideas. Like other MTLD militants, Krim was disconcerted by the quarrel between Messali and the Central Committee. When there was no hope of reconciliation, he played a leading rôle in forming a 'third force', the CRUA. For some time after the outbreak of the rebellion, Krim headed the Kabyle *Wilaya*, then took command of the whole military effort. Fearless and decisive in his military decisions, Krim had little experience or knowledge of international politics before he set up a headquarters in Tunis in 1957.

Ben Bella was born in Oran in western Algeria of Moroccan parents. Like Krim, he was a soldier in the French Army before taking up nationalist activities in earnest. He was decorated for bravery in the North African and Italian campaigns during World War II. In 1946, he returned home and was elected to the Municipal Council of his native town. He soon became deeply involved in MTLD activities throughout the Oran Province and, in 1949, succeeded Hussein Ait Ahmed as chief of the para-military Special Organization. When the French police uncovered the OS in 1950, Ben Bella was arrested. Escaping from prison in 1952, he found his way to Cairo, where he founded an MTLD headquarters and worked with the Committee for the Liberation of the Maghreb. Like Krim, Ben Bella was concerned by the growing split in MTLD ranks. Through Boudiaf, he established contact with the internal leaders and planned the revolt. Handsome and magnetic, Ben Bella is credited with exceptional organizational ability. He was responsible for obtaining vital arms from somewhat reluctant foreign governments and shipping them to the *maquis* over devious routes. In 1956 his External Delegation had gone a long way toward a negotiated solution with France when he was suddenly captured. A Moroccan plane carrying the delegation to Tunis for final North African consultations was diverted to Algiers by French military intelligence. Although his imprisonment has diminished his influence on the course of the Rebellion, the naming of Ben Bella as First Deputy Prime Minister seems to indicate he has retained considerable prestige.

Most Algerians who gained leadership experience either in the legal period of Algerian nationalism or in the French Army are now participating in some phase of the Rebellion. The majority belongs to the generation, born in the 1920s, whose main view of France was one of internal division and catastrophic defeat in 1940. Though it has some French education, this generation had little experience of fruitful co-operation with France, unlike Abbas' generation, whose youthful ideal was to be Frenchmen of the Islamic faith. The rôle of circumstances, such as death or imprisonment, military experience or language ability, has been determinate in the placing of Algerian leaders in particular tasks. Indeed, some of the most extraordinary personalities of the rebellion, such as Ben Boulaid, Ben M'Hidi and Abane, are now dead. Ben Boulaid remains a hero to the *maquisards* of the Aurès and his picture still hangs on many walls deep in the mountains. Ben Boulaid gave both his financial resources – made from the transport business – and his organizational talent to the Rebellion. Without them, it is possible that the revolt in this key turbulent area might not have been successful. Short of supplies and ammunition in early 1955, he went in search of them and was captured by the French at the Libyan frontier. In November, he made a spectacular escape and returned to his *Wilaya*. Mystery still surrounds the circumstances of the death of the 'Father of the Aurès'. Ben M'Hidi, the organizer of the Oran *Wilaya*, is already a legendary figure in the history of the Rebellion. He is one of the few top leaders to be captured and tortured to death by the French. A cultured intellect, an original thinker and theoretician of rebellion, he argued fervently for his cause with the paratroop Colonel who finally put him to death. Said Ben M'Hidi:

> Colonel, we are, you and I, 'gentlemen' because we scorn death, but you, you will be defeated because you do not believe in anything. Frenchmen no longer believe in France. You are the past, you are divided, you do not know what you want, we, we are the future. We believe in the Algerian Republic. If I die, thousands will come after me to fight. . . .'[2]

Abane, a Kabyle politician, was perhaps the most forceful personality of the Algerian Rebellion. From October 1956 until his death in February 1958 he impressed his energy and un-compromising determination upon the revolt with an iron hand. A Leninist-type revolutionary *par excellence*, he believed in the value of a terrorist act in a large city. Said Abane: 'A curfew in Algiers is worth two hundred dead in the mountains.' Abane was a man of extreme subtlety and high organizational talent; he travelled everywhere in Algeria, linking up the *maquis* and improving methods. On just such a trip, he was killed outright in a French ambush.

Characterizations of Algerian leadership as political *versus* military, intransigent *versus* compromising, or Kabyle Berber *versus* Arab, while descriptive, do not appear to be essentially meaningful in the long term. Despite their wide dispersal and obvious differences of views, the common struggle against France has provided a unifying force which has rallied all but a very few of the leaders to decisions taken by the majority. Algerian leadership is then in a collective phase: a phase which will end with the Rebellion. The leadership is also essentially replaceable and interchangeable, for many of its members, even those of secondary rank, appear to have the capacities presently demanded. And the end of the war will bring un-known leaders down from the mountains, although it is not likely they will entirely eclipse the present ones.

STRUCTURE OF THE FRONT OF NATIONAL LIBERATION

At the top of the Front-Army structure, the military and political leaders and functions are highly integrated. Indeed, the Front includes the principles on its two governing bodies. This is also true in the new Provisional Government. At lower levels, however, the organizations of the Front and the Army, while still closely connected, are somewhat more distinct. At all levels of the Army, political commissars or instructors are attached to the military commands and have the same rank as their military counterparts. The political commissars are in charge, not only of preparing the ground for a military operation through propaganda and informational activities, but also of setting up local administrations to take care of non-military problems during the Army's stay in a given area and thereafter. The basic effort of the Front within this sphere has been to establish a State within a State, performing for the Algerians, in secret or in the open in liberated areas, all of the functions previously performed by the French administration.

In each village, the political commissars are responsible for setting up Popular Assemblies. Just as the FLN rejects the 'cult of the personality' in the top leadership, so at the bottom the leadership is also collective. The main functions of this leadership are to create close ties between the rebel forces and the people, to mobilize the area for war, and to fill all local needs. The Popular Assemblies are elected and presided over by a President responsible for civil matters and the transmitting of local complaints to higher authorities. Each decision is, however, taken in common by the entire Assembly. A second member is responsible for financial matters, the collection of taxes on the basis of 'ability to pay' and the proper use of these funds. A third official is responsible for information and propaganda. He distributes Front and Army news, builds morale, seeks out and denounces traitors, assures mail distribution and rapid communication, and also takes charge of elementary education. This official is the local auxiliary of the political commissar in the overall area. Another official is responsible for food and supplies; the fifth member for police and security matters. He is empowered to call upon the Army's police if necessary. He directs certain vital activities of the village such as distribution of water, and organizes passive defence against the French authorities. He provides immediate information to the Front, conceals rebels in the village when necessary and sets up meetings to take place within the area.

STRUCTURE OF THE ARMY OF NATIONAL LIBERATION

The Army of National Liberation is the backbone of the Algerian Revolution: without it no political effort would be meaningful. In the early months of the Rebellion, the Army was no more than a group of bands operating pretty much on their own and raiding the French Army for most of their guns and ammunition. By August 1956 the Army was able to reorganize and assign its various units to specific tasks at the Soummam Valley conference. That conference divided Algeria into six *Wilayas*, based on the old political divisions. The *Wilayas* have not always had the same boundaries and activity in each zone has varied greatly. To the original five was added the *Wilaya* of the Sahara. The city of Algiers was considered an autonomous zone within *Wilaya* IV (Algerois), because of the special problems existing there; and, during the course of 1957, the Base of the East and the Base of the West were organized on the Algerian-Tunisian and the Algerian-Moroccan borders respectively to deal with the flow of arms and men in these two areas.

Each *Wilaya* is divided, according to the Soummam decision, into zones; each zone into regions; each region into sectors. Each Army Command Post has a political-military leader and three assistants for military, political and intelligence and liaison work. At the *Wilaya* level, the commander holds the rank of colonel, the highest rank the Army will use until independence. Military units were also standardized at Soummam: the group (*fauj*) of eleven men; the section (*ferka*) of thirty-five men; the company (*katiba*) of 110 men; and the battalion (*failek*) of 350 men. The conference provided for adoption by the Army as a whole of the ten grades already existing in the Kabyle *maquis*, running from corporal to colonel. A pay scale was established ranging from 1000 francs per month (about $2 at present exchange rates) for the average soldier to 5000 francs per month for a colonel. But many men fight without pay. Provision was also made for family allowances and for relief to families of prisoners and war dead.

Writing about the Army in November 1957, the Front newspaper *El Moudjahid* confirmed the general outline of organization as set down at the Soummam conference. It declared: 'The ALN is an organized and regular army equipped in the modern fashion.' 'The secret of the effectiveness and the power of the ALN resides essentially in the unconditional support given to it by the population.' There are three types of volunteers in the Army ranks: the *Moudjahidines* (freedom fighters or combatants of the faith), the *Moussebelines* (auxiliaries), and the *Fidaiyines* (city fighters). In some areas, large numbers of 'commandos of death', also called *Moussebelines*, operate independently of the local command and undertake especially dangerous missions. The Army had by 1957 established several central services, including health services with dispensaries and hospitals, liaison with other commands, social services for victims and their families, propaganda, information and education, and extended the activities of the political commissars.

During 1958 the Algerian Army was progressively transformed from the 'revolutionary' force of the early days to a more regular army. At first, all-comers had been accepted to swell the ranks, but gradually most freebooters and adventurers had been killed in battle or disappeared. Recruitment became selective and a premium was placed on previous military experience. Classes in tactics and discipline were given in the *maquis* itself, while more extensive courses for both officers and men were held in camps in Tunisia and Morocco. Some trainees went as far as Egypt for commando courses and to East Germany or Baghdad for jet pilot and engineering studies. One symptom of the 'regularization' of the Army was the

'Regulation of General Discipline and Military Jurisdiction' put into effect in all the *Wilayas* in April 1958. Brief and to the point, the new code set out punishments for simple breaches (bad character, quarrelling, laziness . . .), serious breaches (attempted murder, loss of arms, theft, drunkenness . . .) and very serious breaches of discipline (desertion, dissidence and rebellion, treason, cowardice in the face of the enemy, adultery . . .). For the last category, the soldier is brought before a military tribunal and can be sentenced to death. The first and most interesting section of the military code defines the *moudjahid* (freedom fighter) and sets out his duties and rights. He is a volunteer for the duration of the war. He must have 'anchored in him love of country', 'a total devotion going as far as the sacrifice of his life for the liberation and defence' of Algeria. He must have 'concern and solicitude for the people from whom he comes and for whom he fights'. Toward himself, the *moudjahid* must show respect; he must be honest, frank, sincere; he must banish egoism. 'It is recommended that every *moudjahid* practice the principles of the Muslim religion.' To his fighting comrades, the *moudjahid* owes 'assistance in the worst moments of the common struggle'. To his chief, the *moudjahid* owes deference, total confidence; and for him, the chief must be 'an example of sacrifice, of courage, of justice and of devotion . . .'. 1958 also saw improvements in transportation, although the Army still moved mostly on foot, sometimes on muleback and in civilian vehicles in safe zones. Communications were standardized and each *Wilaya* could talk daily by radio with the General Staff outside Algeria. And the Army was not without its internal newspapers and its humour. Local journals circulated, chronicling battles and sharing the latest jokes.

The size of the Algerian Army and the exact extent of its armament is not known. According to its own estimate it started from a few hundred recruits in 1954, reached 3000 in early 1955, 40 000 in 1956, 100 000 in 1958, and 130 000 in 1959. French estimates gave the Army in 1956 15 000 regular troops and 10 000 additional auxiliaries; in October 1957,

35 000 regular troops and 30 000 auxiliaries. In any case, the size of the Army has been limited primarily by the availability of arms, not men.

The first weapons of the Army were the hunting rifles, knives and other rudimentary arms owned by many Algerian mountaineers. Some arms caches hidden during World War II also fell into the hands of the rebels. During the first year of the war, few weapons came from outside, and most new weapons came from raids on French Army depots. Toward the end of 1955, logistic support improved and guns, largely Second World War models, came from the Arab states or were purchased on the European arms market. In November 1957, the Army still claimed that its armament came 75% from attacks on the French. By this time the hunting guns of the early period were 'souvenirs', replaced by rifles, light and heavy machine guns, bazookas and mortars. During 1958, there were reports that the Algerian Army would get Piper Cub aeroplanes for liaison and observation purposes; but they had not appeared by early 1959. Arms for the rebels continue to find their way into Algeria across the Tunisian border, the Moroccan border and by sea. Arms came primarily from the Arab world and Europe, funds from many countries. No weapons made since 1945 in the Soviet bloc have been found in Algeria, although Czech-made weapons from World War II have been bought by the Algerians in Europe. The first big shipment of Communist arms, if it comes, will be from the Communist Chinese.

STRATEGY AND TACTICS

The military strategy and tactics of the Algerian Army have been inspired by many previous revolutions. The classical texts on guerrilla warfare have been read, notably those of Mao Tse-tung. The French Resistance has given the rebels much of their vocabulary, including the word *maquis*. The Russian experience does not appear particularly applicable in Algeria, but Yugoslav guerrilla warfare during World War II has been closely studied by Algerians, and the Irish Sinn Fein movement has inspired some military and political thinkers. But in the main, tactics have been those used for many years in the Algerian *maquis*, and some have been directly adopted from earlier Algerian revolts. The general strategy of the Army has been to increase progressively the tempo and scope of its action. From time to time, military men have talked of some kind of Dien Bien Phu for the French, but until new arms appear, and make a basic change in fire power, the Army's approach is to sow an atmosphere of insecurity in every corner of Algeria. In this, local circumstances, the strength of French forces and the possibilities of supply have been primary considerations. The experience of some of the Algerian troops in the Indo-China War has not been put to wide use, and most of the high-level Army leaders did not take part in that war. More than anything else, the tactics used have depended on the personality of the leader on the spot.

REFERENCES

[1] Jules Monnerot, *Sociology of Communism*, pp. 302-8.
[2] *L'Express*, 24 October 1957.

Chapter 9

The Revolutionary Years

THE FIRST APPEAL

NO REVOLUTIONARIES are fully able to judge the response to their appeals for revolt. These initial startling attacks of 1 November could not be kept up and the Rebellion might easily have been nipped in the bud by the better-equipped and more numerous French forces. The first task of the FLN was to obtain the popular support necessary to continue and to develop its military action. On 1 November the rebel 'Secretariat' circulated a tract explaining its objectives and methods. The tract, an amazingly sophisticated document directed to a largely illiterate people, was a balanced expression of much of the thinking which had gone on among CRUA leaders. The action of the FLN, said the tract, was 'directed solely against colonialism', and its objective was 'national independence within the North-African framework'. That independence was to be obtained through: '(I) The restoration of the sovereign, democratic and social Algerian state within the framework of Islamic principles. (II) Respect of all fundamental liberties without distinction of race or creed.' Calling for the 'restoration' of the Algerian state rather than its establishment, the FLN made itself heir to the Algeria which existed before 1830. A sovereign, democratic and social Algerian state was an aspiration in terms familiar to French Constitutions. 'Islamic principles', though rare in the FLN's secular and nationalistic propaganda responded to the profoundly Muslim Algerian population. And 'fundamental liberties without distinction of race or creed' touched the deep resentments shared by all

Algerians against the racialist attitudes of the French in Algeria.

The FLN continued by stating its internal aims. '(I) Political reorganization by restoring the national revolutionary movement to its rightful course and by wiping out every vestige of corruption and reformism which are the cause of our present regression. (II) The rallying and organization of all the sound forces of the Algerian people in order to liquidate the colonial system.' The FLN thus sketched its answer to the primary political problem of uniting the Algerian people behind leaders who supported its revolutionary principles of unity and action. The FLN itself would ultimately decide the extent of the 'sound' forces. As its foreign aims, the FLN put forth: '(I) Internationalization of the Algerian problem. (II) The fulfilment of North African unity within the natural Arab-Muslim framework. (III) Within the framework of the United Nations, the affirmation of active sympathy with regard to all nations supporting our liberation action.' Implicit in these aims was the assumption that military means would not be sufficient to bring France to the negotiating table on terms favourable to the FLN. At this time the FLN did not intend to seek the support of any particular bloc in the cold war. North African unity within the 'natural Arab-Muslim framework' seemed to suggest a loose collaboration with the Arab-Asian bloc in the United Nations, rather than any FLN attachment to the Arab League.

The FLN left no illusions in the mind of the Algerian people as to the nature of the effort it would be undertaking. 'It is true that the struggle will be long, but the outcome is a certainty.' Then, scarcely launched on its rebellion, the FLN stated its principles and conditions for ending the fighting. '. . . To prove our true desire for real peace, limit the loss of human lives and the bloodshed, we submit to the French authorities an honourable platform for discussion, if they are animated by goodwill and recognize, once for all, for the peoples they rule, the right of self-determination.' Certainly France did not up till 1959 recognize the right of self-determination for its Algerian

Overseas Departments. The laying down of the conditions at this early date may have been done without any serious thought that they would be acceptable to France. The initial conditions in the 1 November 1954 tract were these:

(1) The recognition of Algerian nationality by an official declaration abrogating the edicts, decrees and laws by virtue of which Algeria is French territory in contradiction with history, geography, language, religion and the customs of the Algerian people. (II) The opening of negotiations with authorized spokesmen of the Algerian people based on the recognition of Algerian sovereignty, one and indivisible. (III) The creation of an atmosphere of confidence through the release of all political prisoners, the removal of all special measures and the end of legal action against the Algerian combatants.

This series of conditions does not include the word 'independence'. Although the tract elsewhere mentions that the aim of the FLN is independence within the North African framework, France is required only to recognize Algerian 'nationality' and to negotiate on the basis of Algerian 'sovereignty, one and indivisible'. The difference between nationality or sovereignty and independence may be moot, but in the highly charged atmosphere of a colonial situation specific language often becomes important. That the difference may be more than one of words is suggested by the third condition, one which all Algerian nationalists have called for since the 1920s, the 'creation of an atmosphere of confidence through the release of all political prisoners . . .'. The imprisonment of nationalist leaders had frequently hampered normal Algerian political activity. The 'removal of all special measures and the end of legal action against Algerian combatants' would have amounted, perhaps, to greater equality for the average Algerian and a general amnesty for the rebels who had already taken up arms.

Unusually, the FLN tract also contained its views concerning demands which might be made by the French. In exchange for

the recognition of Algerian nationality and sovereignty, the
FLN offered:

> (I) French cultural and economic interests honestly
> acquired shall be respected, in the same way as persons and
> families. (II) All Frenchmen wishing to remain in Algeria
> will have the choice between their original nationality –
> and will, as a consequence be considered as foreigners in
> the eyes of the law in force – or will be allowed to opt for
> Algerian nationality, in which case they will be con-
> sidered as such from the point of view of rights and
> duties. (III) Relations between France and Algeria will be
> defined and will be the object of an agreement between the
> two countries on a basis of equality and of mutual respect.

Unlike rebel demands upon France, which have grown progressively, this official stand on Frenchmen in Algeria has not
changed since November 1954. It is clear that permitting
French *colons* to retain only those economic interests 'honestly'
acquired and removing the possibility of dual nationality in
Algeria would spell the effective end of the colonial régime.
On the other hand, the FLN position permits a reconciliation
between Algerian Muslims and those *colons* willing to accept
real equality. The FLN might have called for the 'throwing of
the Frenchmen into the sea', but did not. The reason for this
moderation probably lies in the long Algerian cultural ties with
France, Algerians' continuing affinity for the West and the
essentially primitive nature of a wholesale killing or expulsion
of the *colons*. (Although policy has not changed, feelings no
doubt have; and many Algerians would probably be glad,
after more than four years of bitter fighting, to see all the
colons leave.) Armed with this programme, the FLN called on all
Algerians to adhere to the Front. 'The National Liberation
Front is your front. Its victory is your victory.'

MILITARY PROBLEMS

The crucial problem for the Rebellion in the first year of its
existence was that of military organization and equipment.

After initial attacks throughout Algeria, the Army settled in its mountain hide-outs in the Aurès, Kabylia and North Constantine, ideal terrain for guerrilla operations. The French counter-attack was concentrated in the Aurès. Planes and tanks were brought in and the rebels were quickly cut off from the people by regroupment of 'loyal' villages and the destruction of 'suspect' ones. The Algerian Army in the Aurès was led by two extremely capable, if controversial, leaders, Mostefa Ben Boulaid and Bachir Chihani. Their mountainous domain was the home of several different Berber tribes whose fierce loyalties and opposition to outsiders made joint effort difficult. After the deaths of a succession of local military leaders, none could claim full control until 1957. But despite the internal chaos, the ranks of the Army continued to grow.

The Kabyle *maquis* developed somewhat more slowly, and was ruled more efficiently by Krim, Ouamrane, Abane and Nasser. After the 1 November attacks, the Kabyles devoted their attention to the wiping out of 'traitors' – a task it took about nine months to complete. In North Constantine, Youssef Zirout, another able leader, successfully organized the mountainous Algerian-Tunisian frontier, and soon made contact with the External Delegation to smuggle in arms. In all three *Wilayas*, the rebels were not seriously affected by the dissolution of the MTLD in early November and numerous arrests of nationalist leaders. But French military reaction was sharp. The Government of Premier Pierre Mendès-France sent reinforcements, including paratroopers, to Algeria in November and December. The bombing of 'disloyal' villages, the *'ratissages'* ('raking' operations) and similar repressive measures fell directly on the defenceless civilian population. But the net result of these indiscriminate measures was to swell the ranks of the rebels.

A second acute problem for Algerian guerrillas was arms and ammunition. The rebels were frequently forced to attack French military positions solely to obtain arms, sometimes when such a raid would otherwise have been too dangerous. By February 1955 the Aurès *maquis* was almost without ammunition, and it was on a mission to get a new supply that Colonel Ben Boulaid was arrested at the Libyan frontier. The munitions problem also led to some bitterness and estrangement between the *maquisards* and the External Delegation. This natural resentment declined in 1957 when the leaders outside were able to ship in arms in large quantities.

The fundamental strategic problem faced in early months was that of extending the Rebellion from the mountains of eastern Algeria to the plains of Constantine and elsewhere. A widening of the revolt was more urgent as the long-drawn-out negotiations between Tunisia and France concerning limited home rule seemed to be reaching a conclusion. The Algerians, already dependent to a certain extent on passage of arms and men through Tunisia, sided with Tunisian *Neo-Destour* leader Salah Ben Youssef in his opposition to Habib Bourguiba's policy of 'independence by stages'. With the signing of the Tunisian home rule accord and the trial and sentencing to death of Ben Youssef, the FLN reoriented its policy and eventually obtained Bourguiba's co-operation in both arms transits and diplomatic tasks. But, at the time, many FLN leaders would probably have preferred the Tunisians to continue fighting until complete independence for both Tunisia and Algeria had been won.

THE FLN ABSORBS THE PARTIES

On the political side, the FLN had to take a stand on the various groups who had not yet joined the Rebellion. In its first tract, the FLN called upon all Algerians regardless of party or class to embrace the struggle for independence. In fact, the FLN was not to be a Front of parties, but a Front of individuals who, no matter what their previous political views, accepted the Rebellion's aims. After the French administration dissolved the MTLD, the followers of Messali Hadj reformed, calling themselves the *Mouvement National Algérien* (MNA) – the Algerian National Movement – and the Centralists gradually joined the FLN and soon ceased to exist as a faction. Continued efforts in 1955 to get Messali to co-operate with the FLN met with no success. The eventual release of Messalists, found not to be responsible for the insurrection, the setting up of rival *maquis* by the MNA, and collusion between the MNA and the police in France, all led the FLN to accuse the MNA of being a counter-revolutionary force. The FLN attacked and liquidated several small MNA *maquis* during 1955, and in 1957, bitter battles occurred between MNA and FLN advocates among Algerian workers in France. The stakes in this fratricidal battle, which produced bitter hatreds and the most virulent propaganda, were not only the patriotic and financial support of Algerian workers in France, but also the doctrinal principle of unity.

The UDMA, the *Ulema*, the administration-supported representatives and to some extent the Algerian Communist Party were placed in an extremely difficult position by the FLN's recourse to arms. Ferhat Abbas, whose participation in the Front as a symbol of unity and of the Algerian middle class was particularly desired, held secret conversations with FLN representatives in early 1955, and by May had rallied to the Front. Meanwhile, Abbas' followers joined the FLN as individuals and the activities of the UDMA were greatly reduced, although the Party was not banned by the French.

The attitude of the *Ulema*, long a nationalist-oriented movement, was somewhat reserved toward the FLN. Sheik Ibrahimi, President of the *Ulema*, and other leaders outside Algeria at first accepted the Front's programme, then changed their minds, and have since fallen into obscurity. Tewfik-El-Madani, a prominent *Ulema* leader later represented the movement on the governing CNRA. Within Algeria, the *Ulema* were restrained in their support of the FLN because of its use of terror which they opposed on religious grounds. As for the attitude of the moderates, even these protested the repressive measures used by the French Army against the Muslim population. The 61, a group of second college Muslim delegates, led by Dr. Bendjelloul, frequently called on the administration to end the measures which had only succeeded in further extending the Rebellion. Few, during 1955, 'went to Cairo' or called for independence. But their refusal to accept in silence the French military repression prevented the regrouping of moderate Algerians around a policy of French reforms and the consequent isolation of the FLN.

A May 1955 meeting of FLN delegates from Algeria, France and Cairo permitted the group to make a balance sheet of its activities and to draw up future lines of action. The FLN condemned the 'neo-colonialist' policy of France and its attempt to 'chloroform' the people with minor reforms. To unify all nationalists against this policy, the FLN proposed that the people undertake a campaign of political non-co-operation with France and sabotage the economic structure through boycotts, strikes and other passive resistance techniques. The action of the Algerian Army was legitimate and 'vital to break the French military repression'. The FLN also reaffirmed its link with Tunisia and Morocco:

> Cultural, economic, historical and geographic realities make the North African revolution one ideologically and politically. The movements in Algeria, Tunisia and Morocco were the expression of a North African nationalism and not of three distinct nationalisms. The Algerian Revolution would seek unity against France's North African policy, that of negotiating with Tunisia in order to better suppress Algeria.

Finally, the FLN placed its liberation within the context of the 'forces for peace, represented by the resolutions taken at the Bandung Conference'.

INTERNATIONALIZATION BEGINS SLOWLY

The efforts of the FLN to 'internationalize' its struggle with France had resulted some months earlier in a call by the Saudi Arabian Government to the United Nations Security Council. The Saudi Government asked to have the Algerian situation discussed as a threat to international peace and security, but the Council did not take up the matter. In April the FLN, whose delegation was headed by Yazid, a former Centralist, attended the Bandung Conference along with representatives of the

Tunisian *Neo-Destour* (Salah Ben Youssef) and the Moroccan *Istiqlal* (Allal El Fassi). The North Africans called on the Bandung powers to make a formal appeal to the United Nations to discuss the question of Algeria and to give substance to the UN-recognized right of self-determination. The Conference responded to these pleas by noting that in North Africa 'the basic right of the people to study their own language and culture has been suppressed'. It asserted full support for the principle of self-determination. It favoured independence for North Africa and 'urged the French Government to bring about a peaceful settlement of the issues without delay'. Participation in the Bandung Conference permitted the Algerian delegation to make wide contacts, but the effect on French policy was negligible. The FLN suffered a second setback in its drive for internationalization in July. At that time, fourteen members of the Afro-Asian bloc in the United Nations requested the inscription of the Algerian question on the agenda of the General Assembly on the basis of the right of self-determination of peoples. The Steering Committee of the Assembly rejected the request, after some debate, on the grounds that the question was one of French domestic jurisdiction.

THE EXTENSION OF THE REBELLION: 20 AUGUST

20 August was the turning point of 1955, and possibly for the Rebellion as a whole. Despite increased French reinforcements and the proclamation of a state of emergency, the Algerian Army had continued its guerrilla actions and spread a general atmosphere of insecurity through burning farms and food-stocks, and cutting communications. Boycotts of French products, such as tobacco, had also been successful. On 20 August, after several months of preparation, the ALN made a series of synchronized attacks on objectives in the entire Constantine area. The fighting was particularly bitter in Collo, Philippeville, Guelma and Constantine. At the same time, Moroccans brutally attacked the village of Oued-Zem in Morocco, and there were other riots marking the second anniversary of the deposition of the Sultan by the French

administration. In Algeria, there was a high death toll among
Europeans; and stern repressive measures were taken by the
French Army, assisted by the Air Force. Of this battle, the
FLN later said:

> The grasp of the enemy forces was broken. The people
> breathed, became confident again. The battle of the
> *Wilaya* (North Constantine) was definitely won. On the
> national level, the proof was given that we could, when we
> wished, shake and place in danger the administrative and
> military machine of the enemy.
>
> In Washington where, for the first time, the Algerian
> problem was posed, the world had an idea of our possi-
> bilities and our determination.

The attacks of 20 August had many repercussions. French
operations were launched against the rebels; there was a new
call for increased reinforcements from France. The French Press
criticized the methods used by its Army to repress the outbreak. For the first time public opinion in France seemed
impressed by rebel activities. In September the Algerian
Communist Party was banned. The *Beni-Oui-Oui* in the
Algerian Assembly refused to consider the assimilationist
reforms proposed by Jacques Soustelle, who had become
Governor-General in February. These normally acquiescent
Muslims condemned the blind repression, denounced the
principle of collective responsibility and were 'led to observe
that the policy called integration, which has never been
sincerely applied, has become out of date. The vast majority
of the population is devoted to the Algerian National idea.'
The extraordinary session of the Algerian Assembly was then
abruptly adjourned.

In late summer and early autumn, the FLN distributed a tract
throughout Algeria giving a balance sheet of its first nine
months of combat. As did many other FLN tracts, this one
attacked the Messalists, and this time the Centralists as well,
for counter-revolutionary activity. It enumerated the number
of dead and wounded on the French and FLN sides; and

revealed that the FLN had recently acquired anti-aircraft weapons. The interest of the tract lay, however, in two other areas. It said: 'The combat against the French Army has not made us forget our traitors. More than 500 have been killed. Some 100 will carry for the rest of their days the mark of their treasons.' In fact, the first year or so of the Rebellion marked the height of brutal maiming of 'traitors' to the FLN cause by cutting off noses and ears and other markings. This brutality resulted from the bitterness with which the FLN regarded those Muslims who helped the French, and the need to intimidate other would-be collaborators. The practice declined during 1956, and since that time only selected 'traitors' condemned beforehand by an FLN committee have been assassinated.

The tract responded to certain French propaganda themes directed against the FLN claim that it was representative of the Algerian people and solely competent to negotiate on its behalf. This issue of 'representativeness' remains even today in the official propaganda battles. To the French contention that the FLN was composed of bandits and fugitives from justice, the FLN replied that its fighters were 99% young peasants who had never been in prison; 1% had been imprisoned for political reasons. To the French accusation that the FLN was in the service of foreign governments, the FLN insisted it had no foreigner in its ranks and was in the service of Algeria alone. To the theme that FLN military success was due to massive arms shipments from abroad, the FLN repeated that it had taken its arms from the French themselves. To the contention of French 'imperialists' that the FLN was made up of 'primitive, indeed bloodthirsty barbarians, inhuman beings who ignore all of the laws of war', the FLN declared that it had executed no prisoners, whereas the French Army could not say as much. On the key issue of alleged Communist-rebel collusion, the FLN stated: 'Everyone knows that the ACP is non-existent in our country-side and that this party possesses only limited effectives in the big cities. There is no Communist with us and we have no relations with this party.' Finally, the FLN addressed itself to the 'neo-colonialist' argument that 'we have taken up arms because we were hungry, we were unemployed and we were ferociously exploited by grasping *colons*'. The FLN called this a 'gross error' and asserted: '. . . We have taken up arms so that Algeria may recover its liberty and its independence.' 'We are Algerians and we wish to remain so because we are proud to be so. No persecution no matter how barbarous will make us Frenchmen. As, moreover, no social well-being will make us forget our lost liberty.' This affirmation of the political essence of the Revolution was directed toward French reform policies, which have been and continue to be based on the assumption that Algerians are hungry, more than they are nationalists.

Encouraged by its military successes of August, the FLN accepted its first contact with the French liberal Press. In an interview printed on 15 September in the leftist *France Observateur*, Ouamrane, a Kabyle leader, repeated the well-known FLN position on the patriotic, non-Communist, non-foreign character of the Rebellion, on the lack of authority of Messali and the MNA in Algeria, and the FLN's obedience to the laws of war. The ALN had so many volunteers, he said, it had begun to accept only those with military training. The strength of the ALN came from the advantageous terrain; from the fact that it was at home and had the support of the population. The ALN realized, none the less, that it could not win the war. In early November 1954, commented Ouamrane, the ALN was 3000 strong; now it was 12 000, and in a few months it could be 100 000 without difficulty. Ouamrane stated the crucial conditions for a cease-fire: the end of all military operations and the repression; the freeing of all political prisoners; and a French declaration recognizing the principle of the right to liberty and independence of the Algerian people. He continued:

We have spoken of the principle of the right to independence. We are realists: independence must be realized by stages and democratically.

It will be necessary, therefore, to organize, a few months after the return of calm, controlled and free elections for a Constituent Assembly, from which will emanate an

Algerian Government which will negotiate with the French Government the future political status of Algeria, and the new ties which will unite Algeria to France.

Ouamrane asserted that the FLN was not composed of xenophobes. But he added:

> What it is necessary for you to understand is that we will never agree to be assimilated or integrated. . . . We are Algerians. This is for us a question of dignity. The great error which most of your political men commit is to explain the Algerian drama only by the hunger, the misery or the absence of schools when its root is in a demand for honour, for justice and for liberty. . . . We know that with the present Parliament there is little chance that we will be listened to. . . . So we are preparing ourselves for a long and difficult struggle. Our military objectives have so far been fully achieved. After the phase of spectacular insurrection (1 November) and of general insecurity in a region (20 August), we will begin, as soon as our material means permit, the third phase: creation of a free zone in a whole portion of the territory, with proclamation of independence, constitution of a provisional government, call for external aid and an effort for internationalization of the Algerian question. How long will this take? We ourselves do not know . . . but we hope also for a political evolution of the French people itself.

In a subsequent interview[1] given by another FLN leader on 21 September, a certain number of details and clarifications were added. He made it very clear that the conditions stated by Ouamrane were those pertaining to a cease-fire and not to the laying down of arms. The FLN would only lay down its arms to an Algerian Government. On the political and military training of army recruits, the leader commented:

> An individual is not recruited in the Army of National Liberation until after he has militated in the Front itself. In the Front, he militates on a political level.

The political training is uniquely based on the national ideology. We are, above all, *Algerians*. Certainly, Islam cannot flourish under colonialism; for some, this may be one more reason to act. But we do not ask of our members if they are Muslim. We have perhaps atheists. We would accept a Jew, a Protestant, a Catholic provided that he has decided to struggle for the National Liberation and that he accepts the programme of the Front.

Within the ALN, students, peasants and workers fought side by side. In general, the Army recruited only those between eighteen and forty years of age, preferably young men without families, and always in good health. On Communism: 'The Communists will not participate as a Party in the struggle of Liberation. If a Communist wishes to enter the Front of Liberation, as any other political militant, he must resign from his party and adhere to the programme of the Front.' Only the Messalists would be directly attacked, while the moderate nationalists, as long as they contributed to anti-colonialism, would not be molested despite their use of inappropriate means.

The FLN leader referred to heroes of the Algerian past, such as Sheikh El Haddad of the 1871 revolt, as the inspiration of the Rebellion. He made an interesting distinction between the revolutions in China and Algeria:

The problem is not posed for us as in China. The Chinese carried on both National Resistance and Social Revolution. We stop in mid-stream in regard to them. For us the second problem is not posed. We have taken up arms for a well defined aim: national liberation.

The FLN spokesman was asked about the relations of the FLN with Tunisia and Morocco. On the Tunisian-French accord of 1955 for a limited home rule, the leader replied categorically: 'We condemn it. If the equivalent were proposed to Algeria, we would refuse.' And he refused comment on relations with groups fighting in Morocco.

The moderation of the FLN position as shown in these two interviews is striking, the more so that its military position in

September 1955 was still one of great weakness. Where did the possibility of a political settlement lie? – somewhere between assimilation and integration, which was categorically rejected and a declaration by the French Government recognizing the principle of the *right* of independence of the Algerian people In fact, then, with the exception of a declaration of indeter minate duration, the entire settlement was negotiable between an Algerian government resulting from free elections still under French control and the French Government. This moderation is also surprising when its international context is recalled Both Tunisian and Moroccan independence were only a few months off. It appears that Ouamrane felt that the FLN had not been organized sufficiently to receive a grant of sovereignty from France. In any event, the FLN was never again to accept elections under French aegis, and never again to show so much optimism concerning reconciliation. This hope for an accord with France reached its height among politically conscious FLN leaders during the French election campaign of January 1956, when French Socialists and Radicals joined in advocating a programme of peace in Algeria.

THE ORAN FRONT AND THE UNITED NATIONS

On 30 September the FLN made its first important break through on the 'internationalization front'. The General Assembly of the United Nations refused the negative recom mendation of its Steering Committee and placed the question of Algeria on its agenda by a close vote. In October, after months of preparation the FLN opened a new front in Oran This *Wilaya*, the largest of the five northern sectors, was com manded initially by Ben M'Hidi and later by Boussouf. These two leaders organized and equipped many of their troops at Nador in Spanish Morocco, where the Moroccan Army of Liberation also had its origin. Later the headquarters of the Oran *Wilaya* was moved to Oujda where the FLN continued to benefit from the mountainous terrain and the sanctuary of the Moroccan frontier. The attack began in late September and early October, primarily in the Tlemcen region. The Oran

Front left only central and southern Algeria free of extensive rebel activity.

The increased military action made the November UN debate on the Algerian question more bitter. The French delegation refused to participate and left the Assembly. As earlier, the French Government claimed the question to be one of domestic jurisdiction. After the rejection of a South American-sponsored resolution which would have deleted the Algerian item from the agenda altogether, a compromise was unanimously adopted providing that the General Assembly 'decides not to carry on its discussion of the item on its agenda entitled 'Algerian Question" and as a consequence is no longer seized of this item'. The Algerians, who for the first time had sent a member of the External Delegation to New York, were greatly disappointed, but hoped that the delay given to France might result in a peaceful settlement, particularly in view of the forthcoming French elections.

The end of the first year of the Algerian Rebellion saw the national primacy of military matters over the political, and the increasing strength and importance of internal leaders over the External Delegation. The latter had not greatly expanded its political programme and had not yet managed to iron out many of the difficulties encountered in obtaining and supplying arms to the interior.

The elections of January 1956 for the French National Assembly represented another turning-point in Franco-Algerian relations. The Socialists and the Radicals, favouring a peaceful settlement in Algeria, won a mandate from the French people. On 30 January the new Prime Minister, Guy Mollet, nominated General Catroux as Minister-Resident for Algeria. Mollet announced his intention to make a personal trip to Algeria to analyse the problem on the spot.

On 3 February the FLN, in an interview in the French newspaper Le Monde, refined its position concerning a settlement with France, modifications which reflected a hardening of the Front's views. Asked whether the previous FLN position remained valid, a spokesman outlined these conditions for a cease-fire:

(*a*) Declaration of the French Government recognizing the independence of Algeria.

(*b*) Liberation of detainees and those condemned for political crimes and delicts since 1930. Return of political exiles. End of the war operations of the French Army. Cessation of the proceedings undertaken against Algerian patriots. Amnesty from all sentences pronounced *in absentia* for political crimes and delicts.

(*c*) Constitution of an Algerian government of negotiation.

He added that the question of elections was a purely Algerian affair. 'It will belong to the Algerian Government and to the Algerian Government alone to decide upon the date and the modalities of the election.' He concluded: 'The Constitution of an Algerian government which must precede the cease-fire, the system of administration and of police on the Algerian territory will be determined by the said Government.' This restatement of FLN conditions is noteworthy for its mention of French *recognition* of *independence* for Algeria rather than the principle or the right of independence. The FLN, strengthened by its military activities, now appeared to envisage a direct grant of sovereignty from France to itself.

On 6 February, Prime Minister Guy Mollet made his announced visit to Algeria. He was greeted by strong protests of the *colons*, who showed their hostility by pelting the new Prime Minister with rotten vegetables. Mollet immediately obtained the resignation of his Resident-Minister designate, and on 9 February named Socialist Robert Lacoste to the post. This experience radically changed Mollet's views and policies, and on 16 February he spoke of 'fixing without equivocation the institutional framework in which the future definitive status of Algeria will be placed: indissoluble ties with the Metropole, but with an Algerian personality'. This was not the peaceful settlement he had advocated during the French election campaign. A few days earlier, Mollet had declared: 'The Government will fight, France will fight to remain in Algeria, and she will

remain there. There is no future for Algeria but with France.'
The French Government now took up military 'pacification'
in earnest.

The reaction of the FLN to the Mollet visit was one of great
disappointment and reinforced determination to continue the
fighting. On 23 February an FLN spokesman stated to the
French leftist newspaper *France Observateur*: 'The declaration of
Mollet remains in the line of traditional French colonialist
policy.' The spokesman asserted that the FLN now represented
all 'honest and sincere nationalists' and that the future Algerian
Government would be made up only of the FLN. Commenting
on a proposal made by Messali Hadj for a round-table conference such as the one at Aix-les-Bains concerning Morocco,
the FLN spokesman stated that the situation was very different
and that in the case of Algeria there would be a Geneva, a
Dien Bien Phu, rather than an Aix-les-Bains.

THE STATE WITHIN THE STATE BEGINS

The first few months of 1956 saw the official gathering to the
Front of most of the remaining Algerian leaders of prominence.
In January, the *Ulema* took a formal position in favour of the
Front. In April, Ferhat Abbas, who had for some months
indicated that he lacked any authority within Algeria, and
Tewfik-El-Madani, the most prominent *Ulema* leader following
the French kidnapping of Sheik Larbi Tebessi, went to Cairo
to join the External Delegation of the FLN. At a spectacular
Press conference, Abbas pledged his support and announced
the dissolution of the UDMA. This act unified within the Front
all important trends of Algerian political thinking, and gave
the FLN added international prestige.

The FLN took important steps in early 1956 toward the
establishment of an Algerian 'state within a state'. In late
February, stimulated somewhat by the formation of an MNA
labour union, the FLN founded the *Union Générale des Travailleurs Algériens* (UGTA) – General Union of Algerian Workers.
Up to this time, those Algerian workers who were organized
had been members of unions affiliated with French unions,

F

notably the Communist-dominated *Confédération Générale du Travail*. The UGTA had considerable initial success, and by the end of May, it claimed 110 000 members. The UGTA asked for better working conditions for Algerians, and its political programme resembled that of the FLN. It was admitted to the International Confederation of Free Trade Unions in July, and has established close relations with the stronger and better organized unions in Tunisia and Morocco. But the UGTA has suffered severely from French repressive measures. Its leaders have been arrested several times; and its activity brought to a virtual standstill. It now maintains a training centre in Tunisia and carries on social welfare work for Algerian worker refugees. Some weeks later the FLN set up the *Union Générale des Commercants Algériens* (UGCA) – the General Union of Algerian Traders, a similar federation for Algerian small businessmen. Both these organizations played important rôles in the terrorist activity which took place in the city of Algiers beginning in the spring of 1956, as well as in the collection of funds to support the Rebellion as a whole.

In another field of political activity, the *Union Générale des Etudiants Musulmans Algériens* (UGEMA) – General Union of Algerian Students – created by the FLN a year earlier, called for a strike of all Algerian Muslim students at examination time in 1956. This strike was effective for some months and resulted in the rallying to the ranks of the FLN of many young students and intellectuals.

The most important political achievement of the FLN during the year was the organization of a successful general strike on 5 July 1956, the anniversary of the surrender of the Dey of Algiers. Commenting on the significance of the strike, the FLN noted that the Algerian people had affirmed:

1. Their unanimous adherence to the National Army of Liberation and its political counterpart, the National Liberation Front, thereby proving that the French theory of a minority of rebels was false.

2. The political maturity of the Algerian people who

will not rest until they have regained their rights to freedom and democracy.

3. The popular character of the national revolution, expressed by the full participation of all social classes in the commemoration of this anniversary: intellectuals, workers, students, peasants alike.

This day also proved that North African solidarity is not meaningless. In the sister Arab countries of Tunisia and Morocco the population took an active part beside their Algerian brothers in all demonstrations headed by the Algerian flag.

In the months preceding the 5 July strike, two events occurred which were to affect the future of the FLN in the international and military spheres. In May and June, the Afro-Asian group at the United Nations held a series of discussions on the Algerian question which resulted in a request for Security Council consideration of the matter. Although the request was rejected, the Council recognized the international character of the Algerian problem. In the military sphere, the FLN-ALN began on 20 June a phase of terrorist bombings in the city of Algiers and elsewhere, which was ultimately to bring the bulk of the French Army to Algeria and which greatly increased the atmosphere of general insecurity in North Africa.

THE SOUMMAM CONFERENCE

Despite these considerable achievements, there was a serious crisis of leadership and organization within the FLN. *El Moudjahid*, the official FLN newspaper, wrote on the issues:

> The insurrection was confronted with a series of difficulties. Far from each other, the *maquis* had not succeeded in making their junction. Liaison between them was difficult, and arms were lacking. The political indoctrination of the armed groups still remained insufficient.

> There was no official national authority. The Revolution lacked a doctrinal base. Often the responsible [leaders] in their separation hesitated to take a definite stand on important problems.

Messalism was still widespread and strongly supported by the enemy.

The idea for a national congress of revolutionary leaders was not a new one. But it found a new advocate in Youssef Zirout, and was later taken up by Abane, Krim and other members of the Kabyle *maquis*. Extensive preparation was made for the congress in Zirout's Constantine *Wilaya*, and after some delay, it was held beginning 20 August in the valley of the Soummam. This valley had been announced by the French Army as a 'pacified' area, and in fact the internal leaders had considerable difficulty communicating with the outside. A number of the leaders, including the entire External Delegation which waited in vain in Italy and Libya, did not attend the conference. The major participants were Krim, Abane, Ouamrane, Ben M'Hidi, Zirout, Mellah, Ben Tobbal, Omar Ben Boulaid, brother of the dead Aurès leader, and Nouaroua. All the *Wilayas*, including the Sahara, to which Mellah had been assigned, were represented.

The congress, truncated as it was, took a certain number of important and lasting decisions in 1956. The ALN was reorganized and 'personalized', adopting the model of the Kabyle *maquis*. It appears that Krim, already the undisputed military leader of the interior, was named Commander-in-Chief at this time. On the political side, the National Council of the Algerian Revolution and its executive Committee of Co-ordination and Implementation were set up. The former body, given overall general direction of the Rebellion, included representation from all parts of the Algerian political spectrum; the latter, composed entirely of internal, and predominantly military, leaders indicated the control of the Rebellion now lay in the hands of those who carried on the fighting, rather than the initial organizers or the External Delegation.

In the doctrinal sphere, the congress set out three basic principles: collective leadership, the primacy of the political over the military, and the primacy of the interior over the exterior. The affirmation of collective leadership showed the nationalists' abiding distrust of a single chief. Indeed, despite personal ambitions, no single FLN leader possessed either the competence or the overall popularity to be generally acceptable as the supreme leader of the Revolution. The principle of the primacy of politics 'affirmed the essential political aim of our struggle: national independence'. This guideline also resulted from the composition of the ALN. Some of its colonels were purely military men with little political sophistication. The political militants felt the need of gaining a priority without which any military man might become a political commander. The effect of the decision was to prevent a captain with no political experience from being promoted to the primary political post of a *Wilaya*, while Army politicians could still fill purely military positions. The principle of the primacy of the interior was no more than a recognition of fact, although it was later disputed by some members of the External Delegation who had helped to organize the revolt and who wished to remain in control of it. The Rebellion was indeed in the hands of those on Algerian soil.

The platform approved by the congress of Soummam, a cardinal document in FLN literature, was divided into three parts: an analysis of the current political situation, general prospects, and methods of action and propaganda.

On the profound changes brought about by the Rebellion, the platform concluded:

> It is an undeniable fact that the action of the ALN has reversed the political climate in Algeria.
>
> It has provoked a psychological shock which has liberated the people from a torpor, from its fear, from its scepticism.
>
> It has permitted the Algerian people a new consciousness of its national dignity.
>
> It has brought about as well a psycho-political unity of all Algerians, a national unanimity which fertilizes the armed struggle and renders the victory ineluctable.

The platform then analysed the political arm of the movement, the FLN, which 'has become today the sole truly national organization' whose influence is 'incontestable and uncontested on all the Algerian territory'. This act is said to be the result of:

(1) The banishment of personal power and the installation of the principle of collective direction composed of men, clean, honest, impervious to corruption, courageous, insensitive to danger, to prison or to the fear of death.

(2) The doctrine is clear. The aim to achieve is national independence. The means is revolution by the destruction of the colonialist régime.

(3) The union of the people has been realized in the struggle against the common enemy, without sectarianism. . . .

(4) The definitive condemnation of the cult of personality, the open struggle against adventurers, spies, valets of the administration. . . .

The platform, however, admits clearly that the FLN's political action was handicapped initially by lack of *cadres* and meagre financial and material means, the need for long work of 'political clarification', and the 'strategic imperative to *subordinate all to the armed struggle*'. This latter defect had already been corrected; and the FLN had had considerable success with strikes and political co-operation. The slow but profound disintegration of the French administration permitted the birth and the development of a duality of power. Already the revolutionary administration was functioning with its clandestine *djemaat* [councils] and its food and supply organizations, collection of taxes, justice, recruitment of *moujahidines*, services of security and information. A new development would occur with the elections of popular assemblies. The presence in the Front of politically sophisticated intellectuals permitted the 'political indoctrination of backward regions'. The platform concluded:

What is certain is that the Algerian Revolution has just passed with honour a first historical phase.

It is a living reality having triumphed over the stupid wager of French colonialism to destroy it within a few months.

It is an organized revolution and not an anarchic revolt.

It is a national struggle to destroy the anarchic régime of colonialization and not a religious war. It is a step forward in the historic direction of humanity and not a return toward feudalism.

It is finally the struggle for a rebirth of an Algerian State under the form of a social and democratic republic and not a restoration of a monarchy or outdated theocracy.

In a section analysing the current political situation, the FLN platform noted the failure of the former parties, the routing of Messalism and the absence of Communism in the movement.[2]

The FLN views on French 'imperialist' strategy pointed out the 'lesson' of the Tunisian and Moroccan experiments. Unable to face the worsening situation in all of North Africa, the French had made concessions to Tunisia and Morocco with the hope of retaining Algeria. Despite its lack of unity, revolutionary North Africa was able to force a change of policy upon France. The FLN concluded: 'in effect, without the independence of Algeria, that of Morocco and of Tunisia is a delusion'. The platform recognized that the serious crisis in relations between the FLN and its two neighbours on timing and joint action was nearing a conclusion. With the independence of Morocco and Tunisia, the FLN gradually accepted diplomatic and other co-operation short of belligerency as almost as desirable as an armed struggle throughout all of North Africa. But the issue was by no means closed.

The FLN programme also took a look at political prospects for the future. The FLN had set in motion a truly popular revolution and the French Government 'convinced of the impossibility of a military solution, is obliged to seek a political solution'. The FLN must follow the principle: 'negotiation follows the all out struggle against the pitiless enemy, it never precedes it'. This position was a function of 'three essential considerations': the need for clear doctrine; the need to develop the armed struggle to the point of general insurrection; the need to engage in large-scale political activity. Asking itself: why we fight? the FLN replied:

I. THE AIMS OF THE WAR

The aims of war, this is the final point of the war after which the aims of peace are realized. The aims of war, this is the situation to which we push the enemy to make him accept our aims of peace. This can be a military victory without conditions . . . or the seeking of a cease-fire or an armistice with a view to negotiations. The result is that, given our situation, our aims of war are politico-military. These are:

(1) The total weakening of the French Army to render impossible its victory by arms.

(2) The deterioration on a grand scale of the colonialist economy by sabotage to render impossible the normal administration of the country.

(3) The maximum disturbance of the situation in France on the economic and social levels to render impossible the continuation of the war.

(4) The political isolation (of France) in Algeria and in the world.

(5) To give to the insurrection such a development as to make it conform with international law (personalization of the army, recognizable political authority, respect of the laws of war, normal administration of liberated zones by the ALN).

(6) To constantly support the people in the face of the extermination efforts of the French.

II. CONDITIONS FOR A CEASE-FIRE

(1) Recognition of the indivisible Algerian nation.

This clause is destined to make the colonialist fiction of 'French Algeria' disappear.

(2) Recognition of the independence of Algeria and its

sovereignty in all domains up to and including national defence and diplomacy.

(3) Liberation of all Algerian men and women, internees or exiles for political activity imprisoned before and after the first of November 1954.

(4) Recognition of the FLN as the sole organization representing the Algerian people and the sole one qualified to negotiate. In return, the FLN is the guarantor of and responsible for the cease-fire in the name of the Algerian people.

III. NEGOTIATIONS FOR PEACE

(1) The conditions for the cease-fire having been fulfilled, the exclusive and valid spokesman for Algeria remains the FLN. All questions concerning the representativity of the Algerian people are the exclusive jurisdiction of the FLN (government, elections, etc. . . .). No activity of this kind by the French Government is acceptable.

(2) *The negotiations are undertaken on the basis of independence* (diplomacy and national defence included).

(3) Establishment of points for discussions:
– limits of Algerian territory (present limits, including the Algerian Sahara);
– French minority (on the basis of the option between Algerian or foreign citizenship – no preferential régime – no dual Algerian and French citizenship);
– French property { of the French state / of French citizens;
– transfer of powers (administration);
– forms of French assistance and co-operation in the economic, monetary, social, cultural domains, etc.;
– other points.

In the second phase, further negotiations would be carried out by an Algerian government, issuing from a constituent assembly after general elections.

The Soummam platform set out the maximum demands of the FLN. Demands for recognition of independence and for acceptance of the FLN as the sole valid Algerian spokesman were repeated. A new element was introduced in the agenda for Franco-Algerian discussion – the limit of Algerian territory which, from 1956 on, became important due to oil discoveries in the Sahara. These discoveries gave Algerians a new hope of economic viability and development but also reinforced French desire to maintain Algeria as French territory. It is of interest that the FLN considered it desirable to carry the conflict to Metropolitan France by creating disturbances there, and to isolate France internationally. Real action along this line did not come until 1958.

The FLN platform also reiterated the desire for North African federation:

> . . . The Algerians will never let their cult of the Father-
> land, noble and generous sentiment, degenerate into a
> blind, narrow and chauvinistic nationalism. . . . The three
> brother peoples have an interest to begin with to organize
> a common defence, common diplomatic action and orien-
> tation, freedom of exchange, a national and common plan
> for equipment and industrialization, a monetary policy,
> teaching and organized exchanges of technical *cadres*,
> cultural exchanges, the common exploitations of our sub-
> soils and our respective Saharan regions.

The new task of the FLN, and the principal doctrinal modifi-
cation which the platform of the Soummam conference made, was the preparation for a general insurrection. It does not appear that this implied a general armed insurrection, but rather the total organization of all sections of the Algerian population to achieve FLN aims. The platform asserted that an all-out effort for the armed struggle and for decisive victory remained a fundamental watchword. To oppose better the 'divide and rule' policy of the French administration, the FLN must:

(*a*) Cement the anti-imperialist national union.

(*b*) Lean in a more particular way on the most numer-
ous, the poorest, the most revolutionary social levels, peasants, agricultural workers.

(*c*) Convince with patience and perseverance the backward element, encourage those who are hesitating, the weak, the moderate, enlighten the unaware.

(*d*) Isolate the ultra-colonialists by seeking the alliance of liberal elements of European or Jewish origin, even if their action is still timid or neutralist.

In a third section of its platform, the FLN leaders at the Soummam conference dealt with means of action and propaganda on the Algerian, North African, French and international levels. Asking itself how it could organize and direct 'millions of men in a gigantic combat', it answered that the best means was to maintain the FLN as the '*sole guide*' of the Algerian Revolution. FLN propaganda must be mature, serious, measured and subtle 'without lacking firmness, frankness and the revolutionary flame'. The political climate must be clarified through further efforts against Messalism, continued opposition to reformism and possible regrouping of traditional pro-administration moderates, and 'maintenance of the communist influence in its cocoon of chrysalis'. Finally, the FLN must transform 'the popular torrent into creative energy'. The FLN platform then discussed in detail ways of getting support from peasants, workers, youth, intellectuals and liberal professions, traders and artisans, women's groups – all sections of society.

As a second means of 'totally' organizing the Algerian population, the FLN favoured alliances with specific groups. It warned that it would be a mistake to consider the Europeans of Algeria as a solid block despite their general superiority complex. In developing the support of liberal opinion in France, itself, the FLN should seek political contact with organizations opposing the war in Algeria, and should obtain financial and technical aid.

On the North African level, the FLN should encourage the co-ordination of diplomatic action to exert pressure on France. In Tunisia and Morocco, it should reinforce Algerian resistance groups which might provide arms. The FLN also called for unified political action through a committee of co-ordination with 'brother national parties'. On the world level, the FLN concluded that the only more or less positive results of French diplomacy were embarrassed declarations reluctantly obtained from the United States, Great Britain and NATO.

> But the world Press, notably the American Press, is pitilessly condemning war crimes, more particularly by the Legion and the paratroopers, genocide of the aged, women, children, the massacre of intellectuals and of innocent civilians, torture of political prisoners, multiplication of concentration camps, execution of hostages.
>
> It is demanding of French colonialism the solemn recognition of the right of the Algerian people to free self-determination.

The Bandung Conference and the tenth session of the UN had destroyed the legal fiction of 'French Algeria'. The FLN platform solemnly declared that, despite French propaganda, the Algerian revolution was not subservient to Cairo, to London, to Moscow or to Washington. On the conciliatory attitude of the Afro-Asian bloc at the Tenth Session of the United Nations, the FLN observed this lack of firmness was decided by the Arab countries, particularly by Egypt. None the less,

> the essential base of our action is situated principally in the Arab countries and in Egypt in particular. Our contacts with the leaders of the brother countries have never been anything else than contact with allies and not of instruments. We must be watchful in a systematic fashion to conserve intact the independence of the Algerian Revolution.

On the international level, the FLN should: urge the Bandung governments to put diplomatic and economic pressures upon France; maintain excellent relations with Libya and Spain (important countries in the logistics field); exploit 'contradictions and rivalries between certain great powers and France'; seek the support of Europe, including Scandinavia and the popular democracies, as well as Latin America; and make use of the Arab immigrants in Latin America. In the future, the FLN should enlarge its external delegation and improve its propaganda abroad.

This section concerning external activities is interesting in that no member of the External Delegation was present. It appears, for example, somewhat optimistic concerning the world Press, and the Press of the United States. It criticizes Egypt for lack of firmness against France on the one hand, and on the other it notes that Egypt is the main country on which the FLN must base its diplomatic action. It concludes that the FLN must always be watchful concerning the maintenance of the complete independence of its action, while asserting that it had never been an instrument of another power. The emphasis on excellent relations with Libya and Spain reveals the concern of the internal leaders about armaments supply routes.

For whatever reason necessary, the congress of the Valley of the Soummam was not representative of the entire FLN leadership. Inevitably, therefore, the absent leaders objected to certain conclusions of the congress and the way it was held. The startling capture of the four most prominent members of the exterior delegation, Ben Bella, Boudiaf, Ait Ahmed and Khider, by the French authorities in late October effectively concluded the argument in favour of the congressists. But the debate continued for several months. One French observer characterizes this debate between the congressists and the imprisoned external leaders as an argument between the Young Turks: Berber, Occidental and proletarian and the historical leaders Arab, Oriental and authoritarian.[3] It is more probable, however, that the disagreements stemmed from failure of the two groups fully to exchange their views at a conference which both could attend. In the argument which took place in secret messages from the Paris prison to the *maquis*, Ben Bella and his associates at first attacked the lack of representativeness of the congress. Ben Bella reminded the *maquisards* that a 'moral compact' existed among the CRUA members that no important decision would be made without full consultation. This compact, which bound others who had later joined the movement, had been broken by the CRUA members at Soummam. Furthermore, said Ben Bella, the nine young men were to be solely responsible for further development of FLN doctrine, and were to keep essential power in their own hands to prevent disunity after the armed conflict ended. Abane replied for the *maquis* leaders by accusing Ben Bella of attempting to become the sole leader of the FLN, and strongly backing the decision of the congress for collective leadership. He asserted that it was normal that the majority of the CNRA and all of the CCE should be from the interior where the real fight was being waged. A committee of internals and externals, which Ben Bella had suggested, was not a feasible instrument to make the day-to-day decisions of the Revolution. Abane's approach to the problem of possible disunity was to place representatives of all tendencies on the CNRA, thus broadening the base of the Revolution. But he seems to have shared to some extent Ben Bella's concern for strong leadership at the top, since he gave extensive power to the CCE, of which he himself was the prime mover. The imprisonment of the external delegates, the publication of the texts of the Soummam Valley congress and other fast moving events made these arguments of little practical importance. The capture of the External Delegation reinforced the supremacy of the internal group. On the outside, only a few leaders of importance remained, among whom Dr. Lamine was the most prominent and also the most closely connected with the internal leadership.

ABORTIVE NEGOTIATIONS WITH FRANCE

The capture of the Algerian External Delegation in the Moroccan airplane on 22 October 1956, ended the first and probably the most hopeful effort to reach a negotiated settlement between Algeria and France. During March and April, exploratory discussions were undertaken between the FLN delegation in Cairo and M. Begarra, accompanied by M. Gorse, personally representing Prime Minister Guy Mollet. Although the FLN delegation also represented the Army, it is not clear to what extent the internal leaders were fully informed about the negotiation. The Algerians made concrete proposals for a Franco-Algerian peace conference. However, no reply to these propositions was received from the French, and it is possible that the French Government considered the discussion as primarily exploratory and did not intend to negotiate seriously at that time. In July, through the efforts of Marshal Tito, the FLN and the French were again brought together during and just after the Brioni meeting of Tito, Nehru and Nasser. The FLN presented a memorandum to the three heads of state reiterating its 'peace aims, . . . cease-fire conditions and our conception of Algerian independence . . .'. It called for the restoration of Algerian sovereignty, the free and full exercise of that sovereignty, national independence, and territorial integrity of Algeria. It considered 'indispensable' the fulfilment of certain political conditions, including French recognition of the Algerian nation as 'one and indivisible', of Algerian independence 'without conditions or reserves', and of an Algerian government appointed to negotiate conditions of peace between France and Algeria. Certain military conditions would also be required. If the conditions for a cease-fire were met, no 'question relating to the special interests of the two parties can possibly remain insoluble'. Beginning in July, a series of five meetings were held between the FLN and representatives of Prime Minister Mollet both at Brioni and in Rome. The main participants for the FLN were Yazid and Khider and on behalf of Mollet, M. Pierre Commin, a prominent French Socialist.

The content of the discussions, which were ultimately broken off with the capture of the External Delegation, is of prime importance since it gives some indication of the minimum demands of the FLN. The FLN later stated in a memorandum to the United Nations:

> . . . the representatives of the Front of National Liberation put forward the necessity for a general political settlement prior to a 'cease-fire' in Algeria. The representatives of the Algerian people reaffirmed their position that France

should recognize Algeria's right to independence and the creation of a provisional Algerian Government with the agreement of the Front of National Liberation, so as to permit the rapid bringing about of a 'cease-fire' and the opening of negotiations to define the relations between France and Algeria. . . .

French proposals never went beyond the granting of certain political reforms which would transform Algeria from a 'group of French Departments' into a sort of large French province with a certain very limited administrative autonomy.

Unlike earlier official demands, the FLN only sought French recognition of its *right* to independence and only asked that the Algerian government of negotiation be created with the *agreement* of the FLN, and not necessarily that it be made up solely of FLN members. On the French side, there appeared a willingness to unify Algeria territorially and to give it a degree of autonomy – an excellent first step should independence be ultimately intended. Mollet's official policy: cease-fire, elections, negotiations had always been unacceptable to the FLN.

The FLN informed Commin of its desire to have 'official' discussions rather than those of a semi-official nature – a request which was granted. The representative of the French Prime Minister also apparently agreed to facilitate travel of FLN leaders to consult other FLN groups. Simultaneously with the negotiations, the Mollet Government requested Tunisia and Morocco to arrange discussions between Algerian representatives and France possibly, including Tunisia and Morocco as well. Commin was informed that the FLN intended to send a delegation to consult with Moroccan and Tunisian leaders at a conference scheduled for late October in Tunis. On its way from Rabat to Tunis, the plane carrying the Algerian delegation was forced to land at Algiers, where the FLN leaders were captured. They were taken to the Paris Santé Prison, where they have remained without trial. Under President de Gaulle's 1959 clemency measures for rebels, they have been moved to an unnamed fortress. This incident, which led to violent riots in Morocco and Tunisia as well as Algeria, forcibly ended the FLN-French talks which were thereafter repudiated by Prime Minister Mollet. The capture of the Moroccan aeroplane reinforced the uncompromising FLN leaders and disillusioned the more moderate ones, who had hoped for a settlement. At no time since 1956 had chances been as good for a negotiated agreement.

TERROR IN THE CITIES

A rebellion must always go forward or it seems to slip back. On the military level, the conflict had to be extended in 1956 in some way similar to the attacks of 20 August 1955, which had such spectacular psychological effects.[4] Military activity had continued throughout all of the *Wilayas* during the months before and after the Soummam conference, but had created little effect on France. The newly designated CCE set up its headquarters in Algiers. If some type of action could be undertaken in the heart of the city itself, the CCE reasoned that a spectacular change might occur in estimates of the FLN's power by French military and public opinion.

From the FLN point of view, the Algerian Rebellion enjoyed its greatest success as well as its most crushing defeat in the battle of Algiers.[5] The organization of the Algiers autonomous zone was perhaps the best ever set up by the FLN and included not only the normal officers concerned with political, military, and liaison and informational activities, but also a special bomb network, committees of intellectuals, businessmen and other specially skilled persons. Among other things, these committees set up the extensive tax collection system which at its height netted the FLN up to $300 000 a month. The FLN organization in Algiers was at the outside no more than 4500 people in a city of 400 000 Muslims and 300 000 Europeans. The military and bomb groups were never more than 200, and the total active apparatus probably was somewhat under 1500. The fact that this organization was able to keep Algiers in terror for almost a year is therefore the more striking.

In organizing its attacks in Algiers, the FLN used every means at its command: the Casbah criminals, informers and double agents, the reluctant Algerian Communist Party *cadres*, students 'out of work' due to the University strike, young girls to carry bombs, and, of course, nationalist militants. The FLN-inspired labour union and business federation provided political and financial support. The battle of Algiers began on 20 September 1956. One bomb exploded in the Milk Bar and a second in the Cafeteria of Michelet Street resulting in three deaths and forty-six other casualties. By this time, the FLN had gained control of the Casbah and set up a small bomb 'factory' with initial Communist assistance.

The bombings in Algiers continued for some months and created a tense atmosphere of insecurity. The terrorism brought General Jacques Massu and his crack 10th Paratroop Division to the city in January 1957. The final result of the battle was a serious defeat for the FLN. Its bomb caches were discovered, its militants arrested and some of its most capable leaders, including Ben M'Hidi of the CCE, were arrested and executed. Although there was never any disagreement on the use of terrorism – that debate ended when the revolt began, some FLN leaders now consider the Algiers operation to have been a mistake. In the later months of the battle, the Casbah was completely cut off by barbed wire from the rest of the city and patrolled day and night. The cost in human life on the FLN side was very great. The FLN found that it had no defence to provide the civilian population against the repressive measures of the paratroopers. It is none the less true that the battle of Algiers brought world attention to the Algerian Rebellion in a striking way. In this, the brutality involved in placing bombs in public places where their explosion inevitably claimed innocent victims seems to have been outweighed by revised estimates of the power of the FLN. On the French side, the tortures used by the paratroopers to obtain information about FLN activities in the city brought on a virtual moral crisis in France. The extreme discontent of the French Army, which overflowed in May 1958, resulted not only from fighting a frustrating guerrilla war on FLN terms, guard duties and other civilian functions, but also from the use of these methods which touched its own conscience deeply.

THE LOGISTICS PROBLEM SOLVED

A second military problem, which became acute at the end of 1956 was the virtual anarchy in the zones bordering on Tunisia. Disorganization in foreign arms support had followed the arrest of the External Delegation. To end the chaos, the CCE ordered Dr. Lamine to Tunis from Cairo to assume the presidency of the External Delegation. From the *maquis* itself, Ouamrane was sent to Tunisia to organize the flow of arms, as Ben Bella had done previously.

The Tunisian Government, headed by President Bourguiba, had scarcely been independent for six months, and was still struggling with problems of internal subversion when it was confronted with a great influx of Algerians, both refugees and rebel fighters, and competing demands for recognition and assistance. It was to the interest of both the Tunisian Government and the FLN to come to some accord – which was reached in February 1957 between President Bourguiba and Ouamrane.[6] The accord, along with certain military actions, permitted the CCE to re-establish direct FLN control in the important border areas. Early in 1957, the CCE nominated Mahmoud Cherif to be its leader in the Aurès, one of the still chaotic *Wilayas*.

Ouamrane then set about obtaining arms from abroad. In a letter to the CCE, Ben Bella had given a balance sheet of arms shipments up to the time of his arrest. About 8000 weapons had already been transported or were in the process of transportation to the *maquis*, a part in Libya, a part in Tunisia and some via Oran. In picking up the various threads of Ben Bella's logistics network, Ouamrane went from Tunis to other countries of the Middle East and Europe. In this work he appears to have disposed of a budget of several billion francs. He also probably received for a time, during and after the Suez crisis, assistance from North African Islamic groups.

1957: ALGERIA'S YEAR AT THE UNITED NATIONS

The failure of FLN-French negotiations during 1956, the serious-ness of the military situation and the Suez crisis all helped make 1957 Algeria's year to be twice discussed at the United Nations. In early October, several Afro-Asian countries called for the placing of the Algerian question on the agenda of the eleventh session of the UN General Assembly. On 12 November, the FLN submitted a memorandum to the President of the General Assembly justifying the need for UN consideration. It stated:

> The Algerians, favouring a peaceful solution by direct negotiations between themselves and France, consider that only the pressure of international public opinion, expressed through the General Assembly of the United Nations, can bring France to accept negotiations with the true repre-sentatives of the Algerian people and a peaceful solution of the Algerian problem.

The memorandum also referred to the support of Tunisia and Morocco and placed the Algerian question in its North African context. During early February, the Political Committee debated Algeria, with the Syrian representative speaking for the FLN. The FLN undertook wide efforts to inform interested delegations of its point of view. On 15 February the General Assembly adopted unanimously a compromise resolution which expressed 'the hope that, in a spirit of co-operation, a peaceful, democratic and just solution will be found by appropriate means in conformity with the Charter of the United Nations'. While the resolution did not call for independence, the question of Algeria had at long last been discussed by the United Nations. The *Algerian Resistance*, the FLN newspaper which had been appearing for about seven months, commented with satis-faction that the objective of internationalization had been achieved and that the competence of the UN to discuss Algeria had been recognized. Seventy-seven nations gave France a delay, it noted, but not to ameliorate the situation militarily. Rather, from then on the United Nations would have a 'right to oversee' the Franco-Algerian conflict. The Afro-Asian resolution, more in conformity with FLN views, was rejected by only one vote in the Political Committee, and the paragraph concerning the right of the Algerian people to self-determination had been adopted.

THE AUTUMN OFFENSIVE AND THE SAHARAN FRONT

The February UN debate on the Algerian question indicated the third year of the Rebellion was to be dominated by political and international developments. None the less, the FLN was faced with new and continuing military problems. The loss of the battle of Algiers and need for internal reorganization made the military front one of considerable difficulties. As earlier, the FLN required some extensive or spectacular demonstration of its continuing ability to resist a reinforced French Army. Military reorganization by its very nature could only be achieved slowly. Disorganized by the battle of Algiers, the CCE found its way to Tunisia in the middle of the year. Wide extension of activity throughout Algeria had produced a need for co-ordination and an improved communications network. The reorganization included such measures as changes in the size and composition of Army units, training in communications, and greater use of Tunisian and Moroccan border areas to carry on basic training. The FLN also decided upon an autumn offensive throughout Algeria, but particularly in the Saharan region heretofore dormant. In October the offensive was launched, but only a few spectacular engagements occurred in the Sahara. From the political point of view, however, this offensive was an important demonstration of the FLN's intention to claim as its own the newly discovered oil resources of the desert. The French Government, for political effect as well as economic, was laying a temporary pipeline which would help bring the Saharan oil to the French market. In early 1958, the pipeline was sabotaged, although small amounts of oil reached France.

THE 'MELOUZA MASSACRE' AND THE STRANGE WAR

In every conflict, there occur incidents which have no military significance, but create strong psychological effects upon world public opinion. Such an incident was the 'Melouza massacre' in Algeria in late May 1957. In one night in a small village in Central Algeria, 303 men, the total male population of the village, were said to have been killed by the FLN in cold blood because of their allegiance to the rival MNA. Shocked by this event, French President Coty called upon the 'universal conscience of mankind' to condemn the brutality. The facts in the case have not yet been fully revealed. No outside observer was able to count the dead, and the incident apparently did not occur in Melouza itself, but in a small village nearby. The FLN accused the French of instigating the massacre, and the MNA Secretary-General later implied that the French were indeed implicated. The FLN called on the United Nations Secretary-General to urge France to permit an investigation. The French Government did not accept, and after much discussion in the Press, the Melouza massacre received little subsequent attention.

Whether or not the conflict between the FLN and the MNA was behind the 'Melouza massacre', the situation in Central Algeria in mid-1957 illustrates the confusion and mixed loyalties of a colonial war. This area was the fief of 'General' Bellounis, a former member of the Central Committee of the MTLD, who had established his own *maquis* and paid a vague allegiance to Messali and the MNA. Finding himself unable to resist FLN military pressure, Bellounis accepted an arrangement with the French Army under which he received arms in return for resistance to the FLN. This tactic, which had been used earlier by the French in Vietnam, particularly angered the FLN. And it may have been that this conflict provided the basis for the creation of a brutal FLN-MNA clash. The FLN was never fully able to liquidate the Bellounis *maquis*, and its existence remained a sore point until early 1958. Bellounis did not make a political agreement with the French, and refused to rally to the cause in May 1958, when the French Army called for closer co-operation between Muslims and Frenchmen in Algeria. Bellounis became a casualty of the *colon*-Army coup of 13 May. The French later claimed to have executed him.

Another strange incident in the tragic Algerian conflict shows how strong deceit and suspicion become when a war takes on religious and racial overtones. All of Algeria's Governors-General during the revolt have been anxious to show they had Muslim support on their side. Some time in 1955, Governor-General Soustelle, a devoted adherent of integration, set up 'self-defence' groups in the Kabylia-Muslims armed by the French to fight the FLN. Among those Muslims approached were FLN fighters, who joined the scheme only after they had obtained permission from their own Colonel. For the FLN, the first problem came when the self-defence groups, after a period of training, were ordered into the mountains to fight. After a high council, the wily Kabyles decided to stage mock battles with their own comrades, and leave already dead 'traitors' on the battlefield. This system worked for some months, while guns and especially ammunition filtered from the self-defence groups to the Kabylia *maquis*. Ironically, it was through one of the most brilliant Kabyles, Abane himself, that the secret was indirectly betrayed to the French. Before the French could move, the self-defence groups had killed their French officers and rejoined the *maquis*. No one seems to know why this was called 'Operation Blue Bird'. The Algerian war abounds in stories like this one. French Army officers of the Special Administrative Services have been known to co-operate with local FLN leaders, sometimes unwittingly, sometimes with full knowledge, in a constructive project useful to both. Wealthy *colons* sometimes pay 'taxes' to the FLN in return for the safety of their properties; and some have been known to shelter rebel leaders from the French Army.

THE FRONTIER CONFLICT

The frontier conflict was the most significant military development of 1957. Ouamrane had succeeded in bringing to Tunisia ever-increasing amounts of arms which crossed into Algeria during the first half of the year. In August, the French Government announced the right of hot pursuit of Algerian rebels into Tunisian territory, a right which it claimed to exist under international law. To cut down the arms traffic, the French erected an electrified barbed-wire barrier – called the Morice Line after the French Defence Minister – for 100 miles along the Algerian-Tunisian frontier, dotted at intervals by radar and artillery. This barbed-wire barrier, resembling the one along the Algerian-Moroccan frontier, was in full operation by September. To cross the Morice Line, the Algerian Army used Bangalore torpedoes to blast a path and wooden-handled clippers to cut the electrified wire. When feasible, the soldiers drove cattle before them to explode the French mines. Soldiers and a chain of pack mules could then cross safely. More recently, the Army has learned to use a diverter to prevent interruption of the current. The Morice Line cost the ALN many extra days of work and loss of life. It slowed arms shipments to internal rebels, but did not prevent them. This has perhaps forced the rebels of the interior to increase their attacks to obtain arms. The Line has also kept an unusually large number of well-trained rebels on Tunisian soil.

The FLN was able to give an important political demonstration of its internal strength in early 1957. Timed to coincide with the Algerian debate at the United Nations, the FLN called for an eight-day strike of the whole population. The *Algerian Resistance* devoted a full issue to the strike, which lasted from 28 January to 5 February. The strike, it said, would demonstrate to the UN that the FLN was fully supported by the Algerian people. The duration of the strike, eight days, which had never before been attempted, 'was the touchstone of the capacity for sacrifice of the people, resulting from its degree of political consciousness'. Some Algerian leaders consider the length of the strike to have been the only serious political error made by Abane. General Massu allowed pillage and took other severe measures during the eight-day period, which brought real loss and hardship to the people.

The FLN extended its Press and propaganda activities during 1957. In the spring, Radio Free Algeria began to broadcast from within Algeria itself, supplementing broadcasts already carried for some time by Radio Cairo and Radio Tunis. In the middle of the year, the *Algerian Resistance* and the *Freedom Fighter* were amalgamated, and thereafter the latter served as the sole newspaper of the FLN. The tone of the Press became increasingly sophisticated, particularly after Ahmed Boumendjel, a former UDMA leader, was placed in charge of the Tunis publication.

EXPANSION OF THE CNRA AND THE CCE

As in 1956, the FLN underwent a reorganization of its leadership during the course of the third year of the Rebellion. The flight from Algeria of all the remaining members of the CCE after the arrest of Ben M'Hidi, military losses and the capture of the four prominent members of the External Delegation had left a certain hiatus which had to be filled. Cairo was selected as the site of the annual CNRA meeting, probably for political and security reasons. The CNRA was expanded from thirty-four to fifty-four members, all of whom were to hold full title. Although the CNRA still appeared as the sovereign organ of the Revolution and its expansion seemed to suggest the ultimate formation of a parliament, its new membership was not made public. The CCE was also enlarged from five to fourteen members, of whom the four external leaders imprisoned in Paris, and Bitat imprisoned in Algiers were honorary members. The remaining nine included both political and military leaders, the latter now abandoning their military rank and handing over their military activities to subordinates. Two members of the first CCE still at liberty were not included among the nine, presumably because they could no longer carry out the functions previously assigned to them. The CCE was clearly to have extensive powers. It was able to consult its honorary members, at least those in Paris, before making important decisions, but the most powerful individuals on the Committee seem to have been Abane, Krim and Lamine, reconfirmed in his position as president of the External Delegation.

Little is known about the eight-day session of the CNRA, and no detailed document issued from the meeting as it had from

Soummam. Only twenty-two members of the CNRA were present. On the matter of principles, the conference reversed two of the Soummam decisions. Noting that some confusion had ensued, the CNRA asserted that 'all those who participate in the liberating struggle, with or without uniform, are equal'. It therefore abolished the primacy of the political over the military, and the interior over the exterior. These changes resulted from the desires of those with military rank to have equal status in the CCE and elsewhere with the politicians – the internal question of political commanders was no longer so pressing. They also reflected the new location of most of the important leaders, who were now directing the struggle from outside rather than within. Only Abane and Colonel Dhiles of the Algiers *Wilaya* abstained on the vote regarding the absence of the primacy of the interior over the exterior. Abane, always a theoretical purist, continued to believe that the internal struggle was the key to the Revolution, and this should not be changed just because he had come out of the *maquis*. But many other leaders, including his Kabyle friends, believed they must retain the control of the movement in their own hands. The second 'clarification' made by the CNRA came out of the long-standing debate between the Westernized *élite* and the more traditionalist Islamists about the nature of a future Algerian state. The CNRA really did not resolve it by stating: 'The aim of the Algerian Revolution remains the institution of a social and democratic Algerian republic, which is not in contradiction with the fundamental principles of Islam.'

NEGOTIATIONS AGAIN FAIL

The question of a negotiated settlement with the French Government remained, as always, the crucial one for the FLN. In the Press and propaganda debate, the government of Bourgès-Maunoury had taken up the theme of his predecessors concerning the lack of a valid Algerian spokesman with whom to talk, and called the FLN intransigent for maintaining its pre-condition of some French recognition of independence prior to negotiations. The FLN sought to explain its reasons for this pre-condition. At the UN session in February 1957 it stated its readiness to negotiate with France with UN guarantees. In March FLN political and military leaders meeting in Tunis held a Press conference. Dr. Lamine asserted that the Algerian people were more than ever 'decided to seize their independence'. Referring to the pre-condition of French recognition of Algerian independence, he stated that the matter was not one of procedure, but one of intention. He was asked whether it was in fact intentional that the FLN now spoke of independence rather than the *right* of independence. Lamine replied briefly: 'It is the same thing.'

In July the FLN was approached by the French Government concerning the feasibility of negotiations. As in 1956, an unusual coincidence of events produced a failure of an otherwise fairly promising effort. The Bourgès-Maunoury Government sent Goeau-Brissonnière, adviser to the Foreign Minister, to Tunis during a meeting of the International Confederation of Free Trade Unions. Dr. Lamine and Yazid of the CNRA happened also to be in the city. Through an Algerian labour leader, Goeau-Brissonnière indicated that he had been delegated officially to meet Yazid. This move was interpreted by the FLN as an attempt to divide the so-called moderates from the more obdurate members of the Algerian leadership. Through an intermediary, Yazid informed the French envoy that he would transmit the French request to the CNRA, but that he had no mandate to undertake a personal discussion. It is possible that the French envoy, who went back to Paris shortly thereafter, might have returned with more flexible instructions. However, the existence of his mission was made public and it was officially disavowed. Toward the end of the month, Yazid, in a memorandum to the Secretary-General of the United Nations, asserted:

> We regret to inform Your Excellency that at the present moment, we do not see any prospects of negotiation or even of Franco-Algerian contact to arrive at a peaceful settlement of the Algerian problem. . . . We have every reason to believe that a *démarche* such as that of Mr.

Goeau-Brissonnière in Tunis represents an official French manœuvre which in no way results from a real desire to solve the Algerian problem by peaceful means, but was planned to coincide with the request by twenty-one members of the United Nations asking the inscription of the Algerian question on the agenda of the twelfth session of the General Assembly of the United Nations.

With the failure of direct FLN-France negotiations once again, the FLN was faced with the question of how and with what countries to organize its continuing struggle. During 1955 the External Delegation had sought support primarily from Egypt and the Bandung countries. In 1956, the independence of Tunisia and Morocco permitted a rapprochement with those two neighbours who were willing to join with the FLN in negotiating or discussing a settlement with France. The capture of the four FLN leaders of the External Delegation ended temporarily this line of approach. In late 1956 and early 1957 the FLN wanted United Nations' guarantees in any negotiations it might undertake with France. This was to prevent the type of disavowal of talks which had been made by the Mollet Government. The Goeau-Brissonnière incident served to reinforce those FLN leaders who had little confidence in the integrity of succeeding French governments. These leaders, therefore, clung to the pre-condition of an official French declaration recognizing Algerian independence prior to any negotiations. But they also saw some value in continuing to sound out French intentions and in associating Algeria's cause with known moderates on the international scene. After a period of fairly close co-operation with Tunisia and Morocco in 1956 and early 1957, the FLN extended its contacts throughout the Arab world; hence, in part, the holding of the meeting of the CNRA in Cairo. Toward the end of the summer, the FLN leaders favouring closer relations with Morocco and Tunisia appeared again to be in the ascendency.

In late October 1957, the CCE met in Tunis and made a declaration on negotiations. It asserted categorically: 'The objectives of the war of national liberation are and remain the independence of Algeria. . . . The CCE deems it indispensable to reaffirm solemnly that there cannot be negotiations without the prior recognition of the independence of Algeria.' On the matter of what type of pressure to be used against France, the CCE 'formulated the hope that in a short time a conference of the free countries of the Maghreb will permit the establishment of a line of common conduct to hasten the coming of Algerian independence'. This reaffirmation ended an unofficial effort by the FLN to give up the pre-condition and negotiate without any prior French commitment. This tactic received no positive French response in any case. The Bourgès-Maunoury Government proceeded to bring to a vote in the French National Assembly the *loi cadre* (framework law) for Algeria. The *loi cadre*, which the FLN opposed as an imposed solution not in conformity with United Nations resolutions on Algeria and a retrogressive step was defeated by the Assembly leading to Bourgès-Maunoury's resignation.

THE TUNISIAN-MOROCCAN GOOD OFFICES

The question of the rôle which Tunisia and Morocco might play in creating conditions favourable to FLN negotiations with a French Government remained open. More and more concerned by the difficulties along their respective frontiers with Algeria, the two governments joined to take an initiative toward peaceful settlement. President Bourguiba and King Mohammed V met in Rabat in late November with FLN observers in attendance. The two governments proposed the opening of negotiations 'which would result in a just solution leading to the concretization of the sovereignty of the Algerian people in conformity with the principles of the Charter of the United Nations' and offered their good offices to this end. The FLN hastened to accept the offer of its two Maghrebian neighbours, while declaring that, as far as it was concerned, sovereignty amounted to independence. The French Government rejected the offer, stating that Tunisia and Morocco were not neutral in the conflict.

The failure of the Tunisian-Moroccan good offices left only
the United Nations as an early recourse for the FLN. On 17 July,
the Afro-Asian group had requested that the Algerian question
again be placed on the agenda for the twelfth session of the
United Nations General Assembly. In mid-September, the FLN
asked the United Nations to proclaim France's 'political in-
capacity' in Algeria. In a second note in early October, it expressed a desire for 'total co-operation' with the United Nations
and pointed out that any peaceful solution must be negotiated
between the FLN and France, that participation of the governments of Tunisia and Morocco was necessary and that a conference of these two countries along with France and the FLN
'has every chance of creating the conditions for a rapid political
settlement of the Algerian problem'. It added:

> The peaceful and negotiated settlement of the Algerian
> problem must satisfy the profound aspirations of the Alger-
> ian people for their independence. The Front of National
> Liberation is prepared to consider any formula of free co-
> operation between France and North Africa, such co-opera-
> tion taking into account the legitimate interests of France.

At the UN debate in November and early December 1957,
moderation and a united Maghreb front prevailed. The Tunisian representative was the official FLN spokesman, as the Syrian
had been in February. FLN strategy was closely co-ordinated
with the Afro-Asian group. The FLN did not seek a resolution
calling for independence of Algeria. Rather it proposed a
moderate draft recognizing that the 'principle of self-determination was applicable' to the Algerian people and calling for negotiations for a solution in accordance with the UN Charter. This
resolution was amended in a manner to make it more satisfactory to France. The amendments were adopted by one vote,
and the resolution was then rejected by the Afro-Asian group,
the Communist bloc and a few other countries by a tie. The
Political Committee therefore made no recommendation to the
General Assembly. On 10 December, the Assembly adopted a
compromise resolution, which took note of the offer of good

offices by Tunisia and Morocco and expressed 'the wish that
n the spirit of effective co-operation, *pourparlers* [talks] will
be entered into, and other appropriate means utilized, with a
view to a solution in conformity with the purposes and principles of the Charter of the United Nations'. In an official
communiqué following the debate, the FLN noted with 'satis-
faction' the adoption of the resolution and reaffirmed its
willingness to undertake negotiations in view of a settlement
of the Algerian problem in conformity with the purposes and
principles of the Charter, and on the basis defined in the joint
communiqué of His Majesty King Mohammed V, and His
Excellency Habib Bourguiba, President of the Tunisian
Republic'. While officially satisfied, the FLN resented the defeat
of its already moderate resolution, and felt the evolution of
United States and Western understanding of its cause to be
too slow. *El Moudjahid* noted that after all little had been
accomplished. The armed struggle must continue, but through
its tactics, the FLN had been able to learn its true friends. In
late January 1958 the FLN again addressed the Secretary-
General of the United Nations. The memorandum noted that
France had ignored the recommendations of the General
Assembly, and moreover extensive loans had been made to
that government by the United States, the International
Monetary Fund and the European Payments Union which
'constitutes a participation in the colonial war of Algeria'.

Events in the fourth year of the Algerian Rebellion, moved
very swiftly. Militarily, the FLN continued the frontier conflict
where it had increasing success in the transport of arms. The
military reorganization, particularly of *Wilaya* finances, and
the improvement of communications proceeded gradually
under the guiding hand of Abane, who travelled throughout
Algeria in late 1957 and early 1958. In February, he was shot
in an ambush, thus removing one of the strongest FLN personalities and an important cohesive force within the leadership.

THE AFRO-ASIAN SOLIDARITY CONFERENCE

On the political front, the FLN considered new ways to obtain

funds and to increase pressure on the Gaillard Government
which had voted a modified *loi cadre*. In late December
the FLN participated in the Communist-dominated Afro-Asian
Peoples' Solidarity Conference held in Cairo. The conference
cheered the Algerian delegation and passed a resolution calling
for immediate recognition of independence, negotiations between France and the FLN on that basis and liberation of the
five Algerian imprisoned leaders. It also called for demonstrations, Press campaigns and other efforts to mobilize world
opinion to denounce French policy. It recommended that the
30th March be designated a day of solidarity with Algeria;
asked for the formation of committees for Algerian liberation
and effective aid to Algerian refugees. The conference appealed
to Afro-Asian governments to defend the independence of
Algeria in international organizations, to attempt to influence
France to end the Algerian war and other Western governments
to cease aid to France. The FLN agreed to participate in the
standing Secretariat of the Conference which was established in
Cairo and it named Dr. Lamine as its representative. The collection of funds on the 30th March in various Afro-Asian
countries swelled FLN coffers and its delegates travelled to a
number of countries to take part in ceremonies.

THE SAKIET BOMBING AND THE US-UK GOOD OFFICES

On 8 February 1958, the French Air Force bombed the
Tunisian village of Sakiet Sidi Youssef. The military blow, for
which the French Government accepted responsibility, led to
strong condemnation by many states. The bombing was said
to have been aimed at Algerian rebels making their base at
Sakiet. Although no rebels were among the seventy dead, the
incident brought to world notice an issue which had become increasingly critical since 1956: the rôle of Tunisia in the Algerian
war. From the time of its independence in March 1956, the
Tunisian Government has 'walked a tightrope' between France
and Algeria, between neutrality and belligerence. Tunisian
sympathies are entirely with the Algerian people in the conflict;
but the young state also wishes French economic aid and Presi-

dent Bourguiba is sincerely devoted to the West. As noted earlier, there was a time when many Algerians wanted Tunisia to fight with them for the independence of both; but Bourguiba felt that, with patience, independence for his small country could be gained by stages and without the tremendous bloodshed of an all-out war. Bourguiba has given every kind of help short of war to his fellow Algerians. At the time of Sakiet, there were Algerian soldiers in Tunisia in greater numbers than the small Tunisian Army. They used this safe haven for training, for rest, for arms depots and transportation. The situation remains essentially the same today. Under these circumstances, the spreading of the Algerian war to the Maghreb is an ever-present possibility. Impulsive French officers, like the one who apparently ordered the bombing of Sakiet without permission of the French Government, could again make a belligerent move against a country which harbours their enemies and which they often blame for their lack of military success.

The French and Tunisian Governments both accepted the good offices of the United States and Great Britain to work out a settlement of the Sakiet issue and Tunisian demands that all remaining French troops be evacuated from Tunisia. For some weeks, Messrs. Murphy of the United States State Department and Beeley of the British Foreign Office travelled between Tunis and Paris in their efforts to achieve a compromise. During the talks, the Tunisian Government presented information and views on Algeria to the US and British envoys. In early April, a compromise concerning partial withdrawal of French troops, regrouping at the base of Bizerte and other provisions was acceptable to the Gaillard Government. The French Assembly, however, rejected the accord leading to the fall of Gaillard and a prolonged crisis.

ACCRA, TANGIER AND MAHDIA

In the interim, important events had taken place on the African level. In February 1958, the CCE decided to establish an Algerian government when the time appeared opportune. The creation of such a government in exile or in a 'free' zone had long been under consideration. But difficulties seemed numerous. To establish and maintain a government within Algeria itself would have been quite a military feat, since the French Army could concentrate its attack on a single site. On the diplomatic level, a government in exile might be recognized only by Communist and Arab countries and might cause embarrassment to Tunisia and Morocco in their relations with France. The ability of Algeria's two Maghrebian neighbours to influence French policy would have been reduced. The February decision therefore was contingent on a proper moment, a moment which did not come until some months later.

In mid-April the FLN participated in the Accra conference of free African states and received their warm support for Algerian independence. The Africans offered diplomatic and other support, including an itinerant African delegation to publicize Algeria's cause. In July 1958, the FLN called upon the African powers to help in presenting its case before the UN General Assembly. In late August several African delegations went to Europe and Latin America to inform both governments and peoples and lobby for support.

At the end of April, the unity of the North African states which the FLN had so long sought appeared close at hand. At a conference in Tangier from 27–30 April 1958, the *Istiqlal* Party of Morocco, the *Neo-Destour* Party of Tunisia and the FLN held discussions on the Algerian war and its repercussions. In a series of resolutions, the three parties 'solemnly proclaimed the imprescriptible right of the Algerian people to sovereignty and independence, as the only condition for the solution of the Franco-Algerian conflict'. The conference thus recognized a modified form of the FLN pre-condition. Moreover, the conference '*decides* that the political parties will bring the total support of their peoples and their governments to the Algerian people fighting for their independence . . .'. And, finally: '*The Conference recommends (after consultations with the Tunisian and Moroccan Governments), the creation of an Algerian Government.*' The FLN had received the sanction of its two more moderate neighbours for the creation of a government. The conference proposed a Maghreb Consultative Assembly which would hold periodic meetings and study and make recommendations to governments on matters of common interest. It recommended meetings of leaders of the 'three countries' to examine the implementation of the recommendations of the Consultative Assembly. Importantly, the Tangier parties recommended to their governments 'not to separately engage the destiny of North Africa in the field of foreign relations and defence until the installation of federal institutions'. For the FLN, which had no legal governmental status, this was a particularly important resolution, giving it the right to be consulted on North African relations with other countries, particularly France.[7] The conference set up a Secretariat of six members, two from each of the participating organizations with two offices, one in Rabat and one in Tunis. The FLN named two former UDMA leaders, Ahmed Boumendjel and Ahmed Francis, to sit on the Secretariat. The conference denounced the 'presence of foreign troops' in North Africa and demanded that 'French forces immediately cease to use Moroccan and Tunisian territory as bases of aggression against the Algerian people . . .'. Finally: 'The peoples of North Africa, through their representatives' denounce the attitude of those powers giving aid to France 'which can only result in a withdrawal of the friendship of these peoples in regard to said powers . . .'. The resolution expressed the hope that 'these powers will renounce that policy disastrous to international peace and co-operation . . .' and addressed 'a solemn and urgent appeal to these powers to put an end to all political and material aid destined to uphold the colonial war in the Arab Maghreb'. The FLN hailed the Tangier decisions with enthusiasm.

In mid-June 1958, the Tunisian and Moroccan Governments and the CCE met at Mahdia, Tunisia, to implement the recommendations of Tangier. Political and diplomatic co-operation was discussed, but the formation of a government for Algeria was delayed. The conferees none the less reaffirmed the right of the people of Algeria to sovereignty and independence.

THE BATTLE OF THE REFERENDUM

The Mahdia Conference had before it one of the most serious psychological and military problems to be faced in the course of the Algerian war. On 13 May 1958 the French Army and the *colons* had defied the authorities in Paris and formed a Committee of Public Safety. The chain of events thus set in motion brought General Charles de Gaulle to the Premiership of the Government of France on 1 June. The Committee of Public Safety and its supporters called for complete union with France and Franco-Muslim reconciliation. General de Gaulle, while not repudiating the movement toward integration, suggested that Algeria might have a 'special place' in a new structure which would include France, her overseas territories and possessions.

In a trip to the overseas territories in August, de Gaulle offered them independence, either immediately by a negative vote in the Constitutional referendum of 28 September or at any time after joining a Franco-African Community. But Algeria was not given this choice. It would participate in the referendum and in subsequent elections, after which 'the rest' would be discussed with the newly elected representatives. The referendum was designed to determine acceptance or rejection of the new Gaullist Constitution for the Fifth French Republic. As a practical matter, however, Muslim voters, to the extent they understood the issue, generally viewed it as a plebiscite for de Gaulle and peace, while the *colons* and the French Army saw a 'yes' vote as a step toward the integration of Algeria with Metropolitan France. Thus 'operation referendum' began, an all-out psychological campaign by the French Army to make as many Muslims as possible vote 'Yes'. The Army also stepped up its military measures to wipe out the rebels.

After nearly four years of war, the battle of the referendum brought to its height the struggle for the allegiance of Algeria's Muslims. As the summer wore on, the French Army, with a firm civil and military grip on Algeria, pulled out all the psychological 'stops' to influence the vote. The Army's commitment to the 'Alliance of 13 May' was a deep one, although its motivations differed from those of the die-hard *colons*. Successively defeated in 1940, in Indo-China and at Suez, where General Jacques Massu had to call off his paratroopers when victory appeared in sight, the Army saw in Algeria its last chance for victory, for prestige, for self-respect. It had no political programme for Algeria, only that it must not be another defeat. In the intermittent Algerian fighting, the Army had been forced to combat hit-and-run guerrilla tactics on mountainous terrain where its modern NATO arms could be used to the least advantage. Insecurity and sabotage throughout the country had forced it to scatter its troops widely to guard every farm, every outpost, every water main and rail link. Urban terrorism had forced it to use stringent measures against civilians and to torture suspects to obtain information. These methods had not only brought on the condemnation of French liberals, but a 'crisis of conscience' at the highest levels of the Army itself. As one French Catholic liberal put it:

> Parliament voted full powers to Robert Lacoste, Minister for Algeria, and he in turn instructed General Massu of the paratroopers to restore order in Algiers by whatever means he saw fit, including torture – without, however, giving him a written order. Thus the Army found itself engaged in politics and police action without any guarantee that it might not suddenly be disavowed by a new government, a turn of events which would have constituted a further setback for it and a further humiliation. It took advantage of the month-long absence of normal authority resulting from the Cabinet crisis last May to try to obtain that guarantee. In its own eyes, its course was entirely understandable.[8]

At the emotional peak of 13 May and the days that followed, the Army grasped at the straw of 'integration' – a policy with a long history and many different meanings. To many of the officers it meant a vague equality among all Algerians, although the economic consequences of equal treatment for European *colons* and Muslims did not receive much serious consideration. It also meant a policy of fraternalization, of bridging the psychological gap which had grown so wide during the Rebellion. In taking the reins of power in Algeria, many officers sincerely believed that their duty had become that 'civilizing mission' which France had failed to complete during the years since the conquest of 1830. They also saw themselves in the front line of the world struggle against Communism: the FLN, following the classical pattern of a revolutionary war, was the tool of Communists, if not actually Communist itself. The Army's view of the Rebellion was coloured by the tragic experience of many officers in Indo-China – some were Viet Minh prisoners for several years – and by the many social welfare tasks it had carried on during the Algerian war. These had put it in touch with the most miserable of the Algerians; the bulk of the Algerian *élite* had joined the Rebellion.

The results of the battle of the referendum: 96·5% 'Yes', 3·5% 'No'. This percentage refers to the division of valid votes; it does not tell the whole story. Of 4 335 009 registered voters, 3 445 060 cast ballots, of which 3 416 088 were valid: 3 299 908 voted 'Yes', 115 791 voted 'No'. From the registration figure, which no doubt includes virtually all eligible *colons* and French soldiers, it is clear that many Muslims, perhaps as many as 1 000 000 avoided registration, even though French soldiers personally visited many villages to obtain names of voters. These non-registrants included not only the rebel forces, but Muslims most opposed to the French régime. The figures also indicate that almost 1 000 000 of those registered did not vote; the vast majority of these and, of course, of those who voted 'No' were probably Muslims. Thus over 2 000 000 Muslims, almost half the adult population, managed to show its opposition to the French colonial régime in some way. The FLN does not play this 'numbers game'. It condemned the referendum from the first as a travesty of the democratic progress. As in the battle of Algiers, the Algerian Army was at a disadvantage: the brunt of French Army pressure fell directly on the civilian population, which was least able to resist. The Algerian Army had the choice of using force against its own population, which it knew to be the victim of the French Army, or of taking a 'do the best you can' attitude. It left the decision up to its local commanders. Most of them took no military action; and the victory of the French Army was particularly bitter for them.

THE FORMATION OF THE PROVISIONAL GOVERNMENT

The FLN was not entirely helpless in the battle of the referendum. From the time de Gaulle took power, the Front carried out a careful strategy aimed at reinforcing its own prestige and creating continuous Muslim confidence in its ability to resist even a strong French Government. In August, the FLN opened a 'second front' in France itself. A series of spectacular attacks against military and police installations and economic targets, including the symbolic oil tanks, gave evidence of considerable FLN strength on Metropolitan soil. The resultant arrests and ill-treatment of many Algerian workers served to widen the breach between North Africans and Frenchmen.

On 19 September the CNRA announced in Cairo, Rabat and Tunis the formation of the Provisional Government of the Algerian Republic, with Ferhat Abbas as Prime Minister, the imprisoned Ben Bella as First Deputy Prime Minister, Krim as Deputy Prime Minister and Minister of Defence and Dr. Lamine as Foreign Minister. The new Government made it clear that its ultimate seat would be on Algerian soil; until this was possible Ministries would be located in the capitals of friendly governments. The formation of the Government gave a strong boost to rebel morale. Legitimacy had been achieved, and somehow the argument about the representative nature of the FLN seemed to have been solved. The French Government of de Gaulle ignored the new symbol of Algerian authority, and by early 1959 only Arab and Communist governments had recognized the rebel régime. As the new Ministries were set up, a whole series of administrative changes took place: as the Army was becoming 'regular', so the political régime became less revolutionary.

Secret Negotiations Fail

General Charles de Gaulle moved forward slowly on his 'grand design' for Algeria as a special part of a reorganized French Community to include all of Africa. In the wake of the successful referendum, de Gaulle visited Constantine in early October and announced a sweeping and expensive five-year plan for the economic development of Algeria. Under the Constantine programme, 400 000 new jobs for Algeria's Muslims would be created, along with new housing for 1 000 000 people. At the end of the period, two-thirds of all Muslim children would be in school; and about 625 000 acres would have been turned back to Muslim peasants. Algeria would be industrialized on the basis of the Sahara's new-found natural gas and oil, and steel and chemical plants would rise on Algeria's coast. Discrimination between Algerian and Metropolitan salaries and other benefits would be removed; and Algerians would have special posts reserved for them in Metropolitan civil and military services. The total cost of the programme would be greater than the cost of the war, now running over $1 billion (U.S.) a year.

De Gaulle's plan for a rejuvenated and more powerful France and a viable Franco-African Community depended to a great extent on bringing peace to Algeria. This logic led de Gaulle to undertake secret contacts with the rebels very soon after he took office. From July through October 1958 moderate Algerian intermediaries plied back and forth between Paris and Cairo with messages. From the FLN viewpoint,[9] these contacts did not involve any substantive questions. De Gaulle invited the FLN to send a representative to Paris for talks; at the same time he sought to explain that his moves in Algeria – reinforcements for the French Army and appointment of Jacques Soustelle, rightist former Governor-General of Algeria, as his Minister of Information – were not intended to prejudice a settlement. The FLN replied several times that it could not send an Algerian to Paris, but would meet de Gaulle or his representative outside France, perhaps in Switzerland or Italy. The contacts were at this inconclusive stage, when the newly-formed Algerian Government met in Cairo to make a final decision on de Gaulle's persistent request to come to Paris. On the same day, 23 October, General de Gaulle revealed at a Press conference the existence of the secret contacts and again invited the Algerians to visit Paris *to discuss a cease-fire*. The Algerian politicians had only to apply to the French Embassies in Tunis or Rabat for a guaranteed safe conduct to Paris, and the rebels on the battlefield could use the time-honoured custom of the white flag. The Algerian Government was angered at de Gaulle for breaking the agreed 'pact of silence' about the contacts, particularly when it had not yet made a final reply. The Algerians were also stunned that de Gaulle wished only to talk about a cease-fire, a proposition they had many times rejected when it was made by the Mollet and other French governments. They rejected de Gaulle's offer noting that they were always ready to discuss an overall *political settlement* in a third country. The Algerian Army's reaction to the offer of a white flag was strong. (The rebels interpreted this to be the white flag of surrender, rather than a flag of truce which de Gaulle may have intended.) Both the Army and the Algerian politicians felt de Gaulle was trying to drive a wedge between them, as the colonial régime had so often done.

ANOTHER 'ALGERIAN' ELECTION

One of de Gaulle's motives in talking to the rebels must surely have been to gain their consent to support at least tacitly candidates in Algerian elections scheduled for the end of November. The French President seems to have understood the notorious reputation which the rigged Algerian elections had gained in the minds of most Muslims. His reasoning in asking the rebels to lay down their arms was that now the peaceful way of the ballot box was again open to them by his new régime. In this, he seems to have underestimated the influence of the French Army and the *colons*, who were by no means prepared to see even quasi-nationalist Algerian candidates win at the polls. The *colons* were anxious to be represented

in the first parliament of the Fifth Republic so they could again
exert influence in Metropolitan France – even though forty-five
of the sixty-six Algerian delegates were to be Muslims. The
French Army, on the other hand, did not believe the time ripe
for elections. It accepted de Gaulle's political decision to hold
them, although it ignored his order to stay out of politics. The
Army produced and supported Muslim candidates who were as
devoted to the idea of 'French Algeria' as were their rightist
colon running mates. The Algerian Rebel Government condemned the elections; any hope of rebel co-operation, if it ever
existed, was lost with the breakdown of contacts with de Gaulle.

General de Gaulle journeyed again to Algeria in December
1958 to talk with the newly-elected Muslim candidates,
although they were not the representative men with whom he
had hoped to discuss Algeria's political future. He also went
deep into the Sahara to inspect the oil and gas resources on
which his economic programme was based. At the oasis of
Touggourt, he said:

> The Sahara must be a great terrain of the future
> between two worlds, the world of the Mediterranean, the
> world of Black Africa, between the world of the Atlantic
> and the world of the Nile and the Red Sea. In this
> immense work, France is directly interested. . . .

About the rebels, he concluded eloquently: 'Ah! the late-
comers of the civil war, let them understand that the page of
combat is turned. Now is the page of progress, of civilization
of refound fraternity. It is the page of men. Long live our
Sahara! Long live France!' On his way back, in Algiers, de
Gaulle labelled the rebels 'fanatics' – he had once called them
courageous. The way to a political settlement seemed closed;
de Gaulle set about implementing his economic reform and
continued the military 'pacification'.

Two-thirds Minus One

In early December the Algerian question came before the
thirteenth session of the United Nations General Assembly.

General de Gaulle instructed the French delegation not to participate, although it had done so at the Eleventh and Twelfth sessions to inform other countries of its position. Changing its policy of the previous year, the Algerian delegation proposed a strong resolution which seventeen Afro-Asian states sponsored in the Political Committee. After a long debate, the resolution was adopted without the compromises which seemed required the year before. In the plenary session of the General Assembly, the Afro-Asian resolution was amended to remove a specific reference to the Provisional Government of the Algerian Republic; it failed by only one vote to achieve the requisite two-thirds majority. In its final form, the resolution recognized 'the right of the Algerian people to independence' – a modified form of the FLN's pre-condition for negotiation, expressed deep concern 'with the continuance of the war in Algeria' – the Rebellion had officially become a war; and considered that 'the present situation in Algeria constitutes a threat to international peace and security'. In the operative paragraph the resolution urged 'negotiations between the two parties . . .'. The Provisional Government was 'fully satisfied' with its victory in the United Nations. Had the order of voting been different the ultimate vote might have been favourable. The FLN noted particularly the 'embarrassment' of France's allies: only eighteen states voted against the resolution, and among the thirty which abstained was the United States.

VOYAGE TO PEKING

While the United Nations debated Algeria, the People's Republic of China rolled out the red carpet for an official delegation of the Algerian Provisional Government, composed of the Algerian Minister of Armament and Supply, the Minister of Social Affairs and the Director of Information. This was the first such reception of the new Government by a 'great power'. Algeria's envoys spent a day visiting a division of the Chinese People's Army, where they expressed particular interest in its various arms 'made in China'. Said Algeria's Minister of Armament to the assembled Chinese troops: 'Algerian fighters have a very high esteem for the Chinese Popular Army of Liberation, for this army is in the service of peace in China and in the world. . . . Fraternal relations between Algeria and China should know a new development.' At a state banquet, Red China's Vice-Premier promised: 'In the days to come, the Algerian people can always count on the determined support of 650 million Chinese.' In reply, the Algerian Minister of Social Affairs emphasized Algeria's determination to gain independence and criticized massive American aid to France. The final communiqué announced that diplomatic and cultural relations would be established between the two countries.

The cordial reception by the Red Chinese has already enhanced Algerian prestige in the eyes of other Africans and Asians. The details of the undoubted Chinese offer of arms and economic aid have not been made public. A Sino-Algerian arms deal could radically change the present military stalemate in the Algerian war; it could bring the Communists to the gateway of Africa. This story is not yet finished. . . .

SUMMARY AND CONCLUSIONS

To sum up, Algerian nationalism was only a vague, inchoate force before the Rebellion of 1954 gave it real substance. It had no real mass following until a few daring young men issued the call to arms. That this nationalism came into being at all was the result of a failure in French policy – and a strong Muslim historical and cultural tradition which went far beyond the limits of Algeria. This culture remained alive, and later began a slow renaissance elsewhere, while it was under severe attack in Algeria. France's failure to make Algerians into Frenchmen would not have been so obvious – in fact, would not have been noticed at all – had not France made Algeria 'an integral part' of herself; and had no Europeans been settled in Algeria to provide such marked contrast to French promises.

The first seventy years of French rule in Algeria were marked by successive military encroachments and the virtual destruction of Muslim society as it had existed before 1830. The Turkish ruling *élite* vanished; the Arab middle class of the cities was dispersed; confiscation of religious and other lands disrupted Islam and the rural population. With the Algerians stunned into silence, these decades were marked by *colon* voices. This strange breed – a mixture of adventurers, speculators, poor Mediterranean peasants and labourers, political exiles – developed its own personality. It was dominated by scorn for the 'primitive Arab' and a fear of eventual engulfment in his growing numbers. The *colon* was more prone to racism than the 'generous ferment of a disinterested culture' and the *largesse* of a benevolent conqueror. The *colon* first rid himself of French military control, then of the regulation of the far-away politicians in Paris. By 1900, he was the virtual master of his own fate – and of the Algerians whom he did not intend to make his equal.

The *colon* had Algeria well in hand for the next fifty years, but was helpless to prevent a Muslim awakening. This came from many sources: the smattering of French education offered to Muslims; the ideas which seeped into the minds of Algerian workers in France; the political rebirth in the rest of the Arab world. The will to liberty that is the hall-mark of the twentieth century found its way even to the Sahara. Algerian nationalism was channelled into two main streams: one within the French system leading to full equality with Frenchmen, the other leading to independence by force if necessary. The moderate approach foundered on the rocks of Metropolitan indifference and *colon* opposition. The radicals, weak and divided, could not get together on methods or timing. But when the spark was lit, all but a very few answered the call for 'unity and action'.

It is useless to speculate on what might have been. In an era when many in the West are beginning to realize the short-comings of nationalism – perhaps because we have already enjoyed it to the full – it is intriguing to wonder if Algerian Muslims could have been Frenchmen after all; or, more relevantly now, whether nationalism can be shortened or modified as a stage in the lives of nations. In any case, France seems to have lacked the will as well as the funds to make Algeria truly French. And since 1954, France had only been

able to 'keep' Algeria by force of arms. The clash of France's
Christian civilization with Algeria's Islam did not end in a
complete victory or defeat for either. Algeria's nationalists now
speak of 'Liberty, Equality, Fraternity' with all the fervour
that must have inspired Frenchmen in 1789.

The Algerian Rebellion has changed greatly over the more
than four years of bloody warfare. It has withstood over half a
million French soldiers armed with the latest NATO weapons
and modern psychological warfare techniques. It claims to
have suffered over 600 000 civilian and military casualties and
the loss of many key leaders. From a few thousand ill-armed
men, the rebels have become an army of over 130 000 well-
trained guerrillas. From an obscure internal outburst, the
Algerian Revolution has become a *cause célèbre* in the Afro-Asian
world and an annual debate at the United Nations. Its
diplomats and logistics men comb the world for support; its
Provisional Government is still scattered in three countries.
The success of the Revolution seems due not primarily to its
leaders, but to the vast reservoir of the Algerian people to
whom it has given a new sense of dignity and participation.

But the *colons* of Algeria and the French have not stood still.
A seemingly endless drain on French pocket-books, the
Algerian war has toppled several French governments. The
progressive abdication by Metropolitans of their civilian
functions in Algeria has now given actual control in Algeria to
the French Army. Fearful of losing another war, the Army
joined the *colons* in May 1958 to force a strong government in
Paris. General Charles de Gaulle and the Fifth French
Republic have not yet played all their cards; but thus far the
determined and perhaps desperate Army is standing fast. For a
victory in the field, either the French or the rebels must change
their tactics or firepower. Such a change is more likely to occur
on the rebel side. Odds and the historical trend toward the
ending of colonial régimes are in favour of the rebels – unless
gradual attrition, economic collapse or a change of heart
bring the two enemies to the conference table first.

The conditions for Franco-Algerian talks are always a matter of great delicacy. Some formula appears desirable – recognition of an Algerian 'nationality', recognition of the 'rights' or the applicability of the 'principle' or 'self-determination' or 'independence' to Algeria – which will both permit the rebels to negotiate without betraying the sacrifices of the Algerian people and preclude a serious loss of face by the French Government and Army as well as a last-ditch *colon* attempt at armed action. With a sincere change of heart and the recognition of the principle of independence, France will most probably find a reservoir of accommodation – now stilled by the brutal methods of pacification – among Algerian leaders, reinforced by the economic necessities of free Algeria and pressures for moderation from Tunisia and Morocco. None the less, any acceptable negotiations are bound to result in some form of legal recognition of the Revolution which has taken place among Algerian Muslims and the resultant need for new patterns of economic, social and political life.

Algerian independence is, it seems to me, only a question of time. What can be expected from an Algerian government in Algiers? First, it will be an Arab Muslim régime, not xenophobic as some of its Middle Eastern counterparts, but not disposed to give anything more than equal treatment to the *colon* who accepts Algerian citizenship. Certainly the vast estates of the wine and alfa grass kings will be a thing of the past. The Algerians cannot be expected to build the *colon*-Muslim community which the *colons* and France failed so dismally to create. Arabic, the mosques, Muslim culture will flourish; French, the language of the nationalist *élite*, is really not the tongue of the Algerian people.

Second, the new régime will probably be a kind of 'directed democracy' – a strong government in which the well-organized Army of National Liberation will have a key rôle. Reconstruction, development, jobs for the more than a million jobless and industrialization with Saharan gas and oil will be the gigantic tasks of the day. Land reform will be one of the first measures; and the grape-lands will most probably be converted to the production of wheat and other crops for home consumption.

Of course, Algeria will need and seek technical and economic aid from outside.

Third, the Algerians will dominate the Maghreb. Dynamic, expansive and preponderant in numbers – not to mention their crack Army – they will no doubt move quickly to set up a loose federation and, later, stronger ties with Tunisia and Morocco. Key points in this new relationship will be joint development of the Sahara – thus avoiding potential boundary disputes – and free movement of people in the Maghrebian area, principally technicians and workers. Political institutions, such as a Maghreb Consultative Assembly are already on the books, but the question of the type of government for a Maghreb state may take some time to resolve.

Finally, the Algerians and their neighbours will evolve a common Maghreb foreign policy. The North Africans will no doubt turn their attention more and more to Africa south of the Sahara – where they have a long history of relations – and hope to exercise leadership in African affairs. Again the Sahara will serve as a meeting-point of common interest. Relations with France will largely depend on how and when she leaves Algeria – and the particular tone of the government in Paris. If the United States support of France in the Algerian war does not substantially change and if the United States bases in Morocco and the French base of Bizerte still exist when the war ends, general Maghrebian policy is bound to be neutralist. But if Western and especially United States policy evolves sympathetically, there is hope for a Maghreb which will co-operate with the West. This is particularly true as far as the menace of internal Communism is concerned. And Algeria will no doubt prefer to receive much-needed economic assistance from the West.

The United States Government has been silent so long about the dreadful Algerian conflict that many Americans have been led to think no United States interests are at stake. And America's continuous support of France – both militarily and economically – has been questioned only by a few small voices – and then, usually after a startling incident, such as the bombing of the Tunisian village of Sakiet. We should not hide from ourselves the fact that American aid has permitted France to carry on the war and that United States bombs and bullets are killing Algerians – the fact that they were not given or sold to France for the purpose makes little difference to those on the receiving end. It should also be obvious that the brutal bombings of Algerian civilians are not hidden to the rest of the world by the cloak of French 'sovereignty'. The Algerians are ethnically, culturally, in every way similar to the Tunisians. And Sakiet has been repeated a hundred times over with more devastation in Algeria. That this human suffering perpetrated by America's oldest ally should have failed to illicit indignation is something of which Americans regrettably cannot be proud.

The human element is not the only one which has escaped us in the Algerian war. Concrete United States interests of both a short and long term nature are in the balance. President Bourguiba of Tunisia has just called on France to negotiate with the Algerians or leave the base of Bizerte by June of 1959. Bizerte is a part of a strategic NATO complex of Mediterranean bases vital to United States security. Of equal importance are the several United States and naval bases in Morocco, where a leftist government has called for United States evacuation. On the dimmer side, no American can fail to appreciate the implications of what Communist penetration of the Maghreb – whether Chinese or Russian – would mean. The Communists on the Atlantic would be serious indeed! But more than the concrete pieces of military hardware, the prestige of the United States abroad, as a leader not only of Europeans, but of all peoples striving for liberty and progress, is deeply involved in the Algerian conflict. What is done or not done will have a lasting effect in the 'most of the world' that lies between Washington and Moscow. The United States Government has thus far contented itself with arguments that its French ally must be supported; and, when the question comes up, with the thought that little could be done to change French policy if it is so desired. Recent events, like Suez, have proved this to be untrue. It is the will not the way that is lacking.

REFERENCES

[1] Cited in Janson, *L'Algérie Hors la Loi*, pp. 295-8.

[2] The comments on the MNA repeated the FLN thesis that Messali and his movement represent a counter-revolutionary force. The analysis of the position of the Algerian Communist Party is more interesting and, using Marxian terminology, in effect accused the ACP of a type of rightist deviationism and a failure to use correct Marxian logic. Despite the legality of the ACP and efforts of the French Press to cite collusion between the ACP and FLN, the FLN platform asserted that the ACP 'has not succeeded in playing a rôle which deserves to be noted'. The ACP condemned 'terrorism' in the early months of the Rebellion because 'the bureaucratic communist leaders, without any contact with the people, were not able correctly to analyse the revolutionary situation'. The FLN further accused the ACP of *Beni-Oui-Ouism* with regard to its subjection to the French Communist Party, its failure to criticize the French Communist Party's vote in favour of the special powers law in Algeria, and its silence concerning the abandonment of demonstrations and transport and other strikes against the war in Algeria. 'The ACP has disappeared as a serious organization especially because of the preponderance in it of European elements, the breakdown of whose artificial national Algerian convictions has brought to the fore the contradictions in the face of armed resistance.' The ACP failure was due to basic confusion and to 'the belief in the impossibility of the national liberation of Algeria before the triumph of the proletarian revolution in France'. This ideology, the FLN asserted, was reminiscent of the Socialist conceptions favourable to assimilation. 'Denying the revolutionary character of the peasantry and of the Algerian peasant in particular, it [the ACP] pretends to defend the Algerian working class against the problematical danger of falling under the direct domination of the "Arab Bourgeoisie", as if the national independence of Algeria would necessarily follow the way of lost revolutions, indeed even to go backward toward a certain feudalism.' The French Communist-dominated labour union, the CGT, was also in a similar dilemma and confusion, and the Algerian workers have therefore 'saluted the birth of the UGTA'. Finally some individual members of the ACP have infiltrated the ranks of the FLN and the ALN, and 'it is possible that these conversions are sincere'. However, 'it is certain that the ACP will try in the future to exploit the "*placements*" with the aim of hiding its total isolation and its absence in the historical combat of the Algerian Revolution'. This analysis of the rôle of the ACP appears extraordinarily realistic and places FLN militants 'on guard'.

[3] The following discussion of the debate on the 'legitimacy' of the congress is summarized from Bromberger, *Les Rebelles Algériens*, pp. 119-38, who uses captured correspondence between the FLN leaders.

[4] There seems to be a rhythm or pattern of development of the Revolution – extending itself now politically, now militarily at the same moment each year. But this is most likely a pattern of hindsight, the natural results of annual meetings and, where the Army is concerned, favourable weather conditions. But one can suggest that August-September are the months for political action; October-November for the opening of a new military front; and December, oddly enough, seems reserved, apart from United Nations debates, for Algerian gestures toward the Communist bloc or Front groups. Secret talks with France seem to begin in early summer and break down in early Autumn.

[5] Factual details in the following paragraphs are taken from Bromberger, *Les Rebelles Algériens*, pp. 139-210.

[6] Sources disagree on the terms of this accord. As stated in Bromberger, *Les Rebelles Algériens*, p. 215, the French version: (1) The Tunisian National Guard was made solely responsible for the transport of arms and supplies on Tunisian territory to designated areas on the border. (2) An FLN commission sitting in Tunis was to provide the instructions for delivery. (3) Those engaged in provisioning the FLN forces were to be licensed. (4) The Algerian fighters were to move about freely only in the military areas along the border. The Tunisian version: (1) the FLN was to respect Tunisian sovereignty and engage in no settling of accounts on

Tunisian territory. (2) The FLN was to inform the Tunisian National Guard, which might provide occasional convoys, of all arms movements, with the particular aim of avoiding clashes with French troops still remaining in Tunisia. The Algerians have not yet made public their side of the story.

[7] In the summer of 1958, a dispute between the Tunisian Government and the FLN arose concerning the interpretation of this recommendation. The Tunisian Government accepted a French proposal to build an oil pipeline from the Algerian Sahara to a Tunisian port. The FLN opposed the project. The dispute was resolved by Tunisian assurances that no oil would run through the pipeline until Algeria achieved independence.

[8] Jean-Marie Domenach, 'Democratic Paralysis in France', *Foreign Affairs*, October 1958, p. 32.

[9] General de Gaulle's version of these events has not been made public.

Postscript

[This section, which sets out developments in Algeria from early 1959 through
the first quarter of 1960, was written by
Lorna Hahn, Instructor in History, Temple
University, Philadelphia, excepting for
'Insurrection in Algiers' written by the
author's brother.]

THROUGHOUT his first year in office, de Gaulle had been
extremely vague concerning the future political status
of Algeria. He would commit himself only to indicate
that 'the future status of Algeria will be decided within Algeria
itself', i.e. ostensibly through elections. By the summer of 1959,
however, it was obvious that he would have to say something
much more concrete. For along with a growing criticism in
France over his failure to halt the conflict was the omnipresent
fact that another session of the United Nations General
Assembly was in the offing. The Algerians had lacked only one
vote the previous year for their resolution; with a new and
apparently friendly régime installed in Cuba[1] – and with
international impatience with the Algerian war increasing –
it appeared that unless France acted swiftly and decisively, the
next session might bring the Algerians a major diplomatic
victory.

Accordingly, de Gaulle spent the summer carefully assessing
public – and, in several important cases, private – opinions.
Visiting Algeria at the end of August, he tactfully suggested
to the Army officers that offering a liberal political settlement
would be the most effective means of capping their pacification

efforts. A tour of France immediately afterwards convinced him that the majority of people would approve such a move, provided it was made to appear as if France was negotiating from strength. He then dropped broad hints to the Press indicating that he would make a definitive move in a speech scheduled for 16 September.

His widely-heralded address disappointed nobody who had hoped for a dramatic pronouncement smacking of *grandeur*. Speaking directly and boldly, de Gaulle announced that he was offering to the Algerian people the right of self-determination. Within four years after a cease-fire had been arranged with the FLN, elections would be held in which voters could choose between three alternatives: internal autonomy, integration with France, or total independence. Although making it clear that the choice was strictly theirs, he indicated that the first would be the wisest, as it could open a new partnership which would permit France to develop the war-racked country. The second, he indicated, would not be feasible, while he tried to make the third unattractive by explaining that France would retain control of the Saharan regions should the Algerians decide upon secession.

This proposal, although in itself settling nothing, constituted a major step toward ending the *guerre sale*. By permitting the Algerian people to shape their own political destiny as they wished, de Gaulle was first of all saying that sovereignty rested with them, not with France. In other words, he was discarding once and for all the theory that 'Algeria is France', and thus implying that there was indeed an Algerian nation. By offering what was ostensibly a fair choice, he was also paving the way for a restoration of confidence in France's good intentions. Finally, he brought peace much closer by, in effect, forcing the FLN to make a direct reply, for should the rebels be reluctant to accept self-determination, they would be admitting uncertainty as to the popularity both of their goals and their personnel.

The proposal was vague regarding the terms of the cease-fire and the conduct of the elections, but it could hardly have been otherwise. To have made specific guarantees to the FLN would have further antagonized an already hostile group of die-hard military leaders, while to have outlined anything suggesting capitulation of the FLN would have killed hopes of a favourable response from the Algerians. Furthermore, by leaving plenty of room for parrying, de Gaulle was giving the FLN the chance to make its own suggestions, thus giving it plenty of opportunity to save face.

Although the reactions from observers ranging from Eisenhower to Bourguiba were extremely enthusiastic, the FLN was in a quandary concerning how to respond. The Provisional Government claimed to hold a stewardship over the sovereignty of the Algerian people, and had been recognized by seventeen countries. Agreeing too hastily to self-determination could easily be interpreted as a denial of its own representative character. In addition, many leaders of the FLN preferred to see in de Gaulle's offer not a magnanimous gesture, but simply an admission that pacification had failed. Therefore, they said, we should receive not vague promises for the future, but instead the victory we have won in battle, i.e. immediate independence. Furthermore, it was claimed, the 'cease-fire' might require the ALN to surrender its arms and retire from the field of battle – moves which would be tantamount to surrender. A further point made was why wait up to four years before holding a referendum, and give the Europeans and anti-FLN elements an opportunity to create a strong opposition? Finally, fears were expressed that de Gaulle might have to revoke his offer under a barrage to pressure from the militarists and extremists.

A majority of the Provisional Government, however, felt that de Gaulle was probably sincere in wanting to rid himself of the Algerian war. Goaded by Bourguiba and King Mohammed, they also concluded that their position in the eyes of the world would be considerably weakened if they rejected a proposal which offered what they themselves had always invoked as their aim. They therefore decided upon a favourite, although qualified, acceptance. The reply issued by Abbas on 28 September agreed to the offer in principle, but insisted that de

Gaulle clarify the terms of the cease-fire and the topics which could be discussed during negotiations. In other words, the FLN wanted some assurance that political matters, which would deal with the method of conducting the referendum, would be included. To clarify the rôle of the Provisional Government during the forthcoming talks, Abbas defined it as 'the depository and guarantor of the interests of the Algerian people until they have expressed themselves freely'.

Chances for *rapport* were increased in mid-October when Premier Debré received from the National Assembly an amazing 412–23 vote in favour of the de Gaulle plan. The massive majority was accumulated only after the government had foiled a plot by several army officers and Algerian terrorist groups to create havoc through a series of political assassinations and fire-eating speeches, the object of which was to force Debré's replacement by the conservative Bidault.[2] The exposure of the alleged plan to kill Senator Mitterand, and the suppression of Right-wing organizations which followed, greatly strengthened de Gaulle's hand, and indicated beyond doubt that he was serious about carrying through his plans for Algeria.

Abbas then announced on November 2 that he was willing to go to Paris to discuss "peace". The use of this word implied that he wanted to include political topics in the discussions, without specifically labelling them as such. De Gaulle replied on 10 November in a Press conference by stating clearly that he wanted the cease-fire to be 'honourable', and by promising that all Algerians would be able to campaign freely in the election campaign. The following week, at a Gaullist Party Congress, Soustelle – who had been touring the Pacific during the *Affaire Mitterand* – tried to force the members to demand an FLN surrender. His faction was quickly silenced, however, and it appeared that the Algerians need not have any further fears about the wisdom of opening negotiations.

The 'Irreconcilables' of the FLN, however, still wanted further details concerning the cease-fire terms before they would consent to opening negotiations. So determined were

they to avoid appearing over-anxious for a truce that they
threatened to break with Abbas and the moderates unless a
firm commitment was demanded from France. In order to
maintain harmony, as well as to obtain further clarification
from de Gaulle, the Provisional Government then issued a
rather belligerent statement on 22 November. Before any talks
could take place, it said, the French would have to promise
that the agenda would include discussions of the terms under
which the elections would take place. In addition, it asked that
the negotiating team be headed by Ben Bella and the other
prisoners. De Gaulle, feeling he had already gone as far as he
dared – and sure that world opinion was already fairly solidly
behind him – could not accept these conditions. The FLN,
however, anxious to avoid an appearance of intransigence on
the eve of the General Assembly debate, thereupon stated
that it would be willing to modify the membership of its
negotiating team. There matters rested as of the beginning
of December.

Instructed by Yazid and other members of the Provisional
Government, the Arab-Asia bloc introduced in the Political
Committee a mildly-worded resolution which 'urges the two
parties concerned to enter into *pourparlers* to determine the conditions necessary for the implementation as early as possible of
the right of self-determination of the Algerian people, including conditions for a cease-fire'. The resolution passed easily on
7 December, thirty-eight to twenty-six, despite the fact that
the United States, reluctant to antagonize de Gaulle, voted
against it, along with the United Kingdom. France, of course,
still claiming that the international body had no right to discuss
what they still considered an internal matter, boycotted the
session. Despite the open opposition from the Western countries,
the Algerians were still hopeful that the resolution would pass
in the plenary session.

When this body convened on 12 December, however, something unprecedented in United Nations history occurred.
When the resolution was read and voted upon paragraph by
paragraph during roll call, it received more than the two-thirds

affirmative votes necessary for passage. When taken up as a whole several minutes later, however, several delegations switched their position. Paraguay, which had voted aye, was now in opposition. Australia, Ecuador, Honduras and Laos changed from abstentions to nayes, while Nicaragua, which had been absent during roll call, now appeared to enter another nay. The resolution was thus defeated by what the French delegation called 'strategy' and co-operation by France 'and a group of friends of France'. The Algerians, somewhat bitter, denounced the proceedings as the result of 'manœuvres and pressures of the Atlantic coalition which, at the request of France, stood firmly against the adoption of any resolution, regardless of content'.³ In other words, it blamed the United States for putting pressure upon several small nations in order to make them vote properly. The United States itself, however, apparently hoping to soothe the Algerians, did not continue to vote nay in the plenary session, but abstained. This did little to comfort the sullen Algerians, while the French, expecting complete solidarity all the way, were likewise chagrined. The net result of the United Nations session, then, was that the Algerians and French were farther from achieving *rapport* than before, while Washington, as usual, was condemned by both parties for weakness and vacillation.

As of early 1960, then, immediate peace for Algeria was not in sight. None the less, tremendous progress had been made since the previous year. Whereas it had seemed unlikely that a meeting of minds could ever be arranged between France and the Algerians, the way was at least open for talks to begin. The matters to be discussed, and the people to be present at the negotiations, were still open questions, and the Algerian refusal to negotiate until they received satisfactory answers seemed to preclude an early cease-fire. However, the Algerian Cabinet reshuffle, announced from Tunis, 19 January, which excluded the 'Cairo irreconcilables', Lamine-Debaghine and El-Madani, and the 'men of Peiping', Benkhedda and Ouseddik, from the Provisional Government, left the moderates in full control. Granted that de Gaulle could remain in power, it seemed only a matter of time before the obstacles to self-determination could be removed.

The great majority of French people were prepared to accept the eventual 'loss' of Algeria – something which had seemed impossible before the advent of de Gaulle. Several factions of the Army, *colon* extremists and their friends, were chafing and even talking of revolt once again, but it still appeared that de Gaulle could control them. Although many observers interpreted his offer of 16 September as a gamble which he was sure of winning, it seemed that instead of trying to seduce the Muslims into remaining with France, he was more concerned with writing off the Algerian *malaise* as soon as possible, to enable him to proceed with more constructive projects.

As for the FLN, it was evidently ready to settle for peace on terms far short of its original demands for immediate independence. This meant that independence would not come instantly, but after a period of preparation. This would probably render the transition to self-rule and the establishment of new institutions, more smooth than had been expected. It also seemed that plans for a confederation of North Africa, with close ties to France, would proceed as planned. In brief, the majority of Frenchmen and Algerians – and their mutual friends – could at last foresee a relatively satisfactory outcome to the Algerian Revolution; something which had seemed a chimerical hope not so very long before.

INSURRECTION IN ALGIERS

On Sunday, 24 January 1960, a *colon* insurrection broke out in Algiers in which 25 Frenchmen were killed and 136 wounded. For eight days, some three thousand insurgents barricaded themselves in downtown Algiers in open defiance of civil and military authorities in both France and Algeria. This uprising posed the most serious threat thus far to the authority of President de Gaulle and, for a time, threatened to lead France into civil war and Algeria into secession.

Early January was marked by a number of developments which contributed to the outbreak. The French Army had been intensifying its increasingly effective campaign of military pacification. Reduced in its military effectiveness, the FLN had stepped up its terroristic activities especially in the Algiers area. The newly reorganized Algerian Provisional Government had eliminated extremist elements which were thought opposed to any negotiations for a cease-fire. *Colon* sentiment was becoming increasingly fearful of a *rapprochement* between Paris and the FLN.

On January 19, General Massu, Commander of the Algiers region, and a favourite of the *colon* group, gave an interview to a correspondent of the Munich *Suddeutsche Zeitung* in which he said 'perhaps the Army made a mistake' in having brought de Gaulle to power, that it might use force against him, and that the President had become 'a man of the Left'. Incensed, de Gaulle recalled Massu and dismissed him three days later on 22 January. This action triggered considerable unrest in Algiers which culminated two days later in an armed clash between anti-Gaullist demonstrators and security forces. Police claim the demonstrators opened fire first but in any event Frenchmen had killed Frenchmen for the first time in Algeria.

By evening most of the rioters had been dispersed, but less than 1000 die-hards threw up street barricades and remained for the night. Paratroopers, called upon to put down the uprising, balked at firing on this group although they were under general instructions to restore order. In the week that followed some 2000 others joined this core of dissidents, arming and provisioning themselves under the sympathetic eyes of the paratroopers. A general strike was called and before long most regular activity in the city came to a standstill. Supporting demonstrations sprang up in other cities.

In Paris, de Gaulle stood solidly on his policy of self-determination for Algeria and denounced the outbreak as 'a bad blow against France; a bad blow against France in Algeria; a bad blow against France before the world; a bad blow against France within France'. As it became apparent that the bulk of French popular opinion was behind him, de Gaulle moved to whip some of his less than enthusiastic ministers into line and to neutralize certain political figures dedicated to subverting his policy on Algeria. Toward the middle of the week, sympathy for the insurgents seemed to run so high that the civil and military commands in Algiers moved out of the city to a secret command post. For an agonizingly long time, de Gaulle refrained from direct personal intervention until on Friday, 29 January, he addressed France and Algeria over radio and television. He told the Army in no uncertain terms to restore order and though he abstained from specifically ordering force it seemed clear he was prepared to go to that end if need be. He reiterated that his plan for self-determination was the 'only policy worthy of France'. He isolated the main European population from the 'liars, the conspirators' and 'the usurpers' who were leading the revolt. He emphasized that the army could put no conditions on its loyalty and that it must obey him. Responding to de Gaulle's dramatic statement, paratroopers sealed off the barricades and next morning the insurrection melted away.

Following the collapse of the uprising, unprecedented punitive measures were instituted against the dissidents in Algeria and subversive elements in Metropolitan France. Implicated military and civilian personnel were relieved of their duties, placed under house arrest or imprisoned. De Gaulle followed through with a vigorous shake-up of both the Army command and his cabinet. Jacques Soustelle, strongest proponent of Algeria remaining French, was probably the most notable casualty. Early in February, the President asked for and received extraordinary powers to rule France by decree for one year.

The insurrection underscored a number of vital factors bearing on the outcome of the Algerian War and, indeed, on the future rôle of France in the Western alliance. Most significantly it illustrated the utter dependence of France on the one person, de Gaulle. If one thing seems certain, this is that the French Government would have fallen had it not been for the overpowering moral and legal authority of the General.

Since his advent to power in June 1958, he had radically altered the institutions and processes of government in France. The Constitution of the Fifth Republic is tailored primarily to fit de Gaulle's unique personality. Much of the previous

democratic character of the French governing process has
been negated or suspended. While these changes have helped
de Gaulle in dealing with many of the serious problems facing
France, they have also made France increasingly dependent
on him. The simple fact is that there is now no one with the
stature to take over the reins of power from de Gaulle. And
without a settlement of the Algerian War it does not seem likely
that an orderly restoration of traditional democracy in the
Metropole could be accomplished. In these circumstances, the
basis of western hopes for a strong France rests squarely on
the shoulders of General de Gaulle, as does any hope for a
settlement of the Algerian War.

The *colons*, for their part, have learned two very important
lessons. First they have found that the popular support they
once had in France is lacking. Without such support they
cannot hope to impose their will on the French Government.
Secondly, although they have some obvious support among the
professional officer corps of the Army, this support is not strong
enough to trump de Gaulle's hand. *Colon* hopes in the insurrection were dashed the first day when the Army declined to join
actively in the uprising. The *colons*, although they have by no
means given up hope are, for the first time, powerless to
exercise a veto over government policy.

The critical rôle of de Gaulle in ensuring France's survival
and extracting obedience from the Army has not been lost on
the FLN. De Gaulle's promise of free elections once peace has
been restored is meaningless to them unless he can ensure that
neither the Army nor the *colons* will interfere in the electoral
process. The FLN has accepted, in principle, the offer of self-
determination but insists on guarantees that the election will,
in fact, be free before laying down its arms. De Gaulle, on the
other hand, cannot give these guarantees without recognizing
the FLN as legitimately representing the Muslim population, an
admission he has thus far refused to make. Although de Gaulle
has now demonstrated he can control both the Army and the
colons, it is highly doubtful that any other Frenchman could do
the same. And so, even should guarantees eventually be given

and a cease-fire be agreed to, the FLN will find itself gambling on the continued tenure of Charles de Gaulle as head of the French state.

REFERENCES

[1] With the probable intention of increasing this friendship, Abbas decorated Castro shortly after the latter assumed power.

[2] For an interesting account of these events, see Joseph Kraft, 'Algeria and the Mitterand Case', *The New Leader*, 23 November, 1959, pp. 12-14.

[3] See 'The Question of Algeria; the Debate at the United Nations', published by the Algerian Office, New York, December 1959.

Selected Bibliography

PRIMARY MATERIALS
ALGERIAN FRONT OF NATIONAL LIBERATION

NEWSPAPERS
La Résistance Algérienne
El Moudjahid

PAMPHLETS
Algeria and Bandung (n.p., n.d.).
The Algerian People and Their Revolution (n.p., n.d.).
The Algerian Problem and the Bandung Conference (Cairo, 1955).
Aspects of the Algerian Revolution (n.p., 1957).
The Freedom Fighter (n.p., 1956).
The Legal Aspects of the Algerian Problem (Cairo, 1955).
La Lutte du Peuple Algérien s'inscrit dans la lutte des peuples d'Afrique et d'Asie (n.p., n.d.).
La Resistance Algérienne et le Front de Libération Nationale (Cairo, 1955).
What is Algeria? (Cairo, 1955).

OTHER DOCUMENTATION
Free Algeria, mimeo., selected issues, 1957-8.
Memoranda to the United Nations, 1957-8.
Press Releases, 1957-8.

ALGERIAN NATIONAL MOVEMENT

NEWSPAPER
La Voix du Peuple

PAMPHLETS

Document on the Algerian Revolution (Paris, 1957).
Messali Hadj, *The Algerian Revolution* (London, 1955).

DEMOCRATIC UNION OF THE ALGERIAN MANIFESTO

NEWSPAPER

La Republique Algérienne

PAMPHLET

Le Manifeste Algérien Parle Aux Français (Paris, 1948).

FRANCE, EMBASSY, WASHINGTON, DC, DOCUMENTATION, 1957-8.

Government-General of Algeria, *Rapport du Groupe d'Etude des Relations Financières entre le Metropole et l'Algérie* (June 1955) (Maspétiol Plan).
Government-General of Algeria, *Résultats Statistiques de Dénombrement de la Population Effectué le 31 Octobre, 1948.*
Government-General of Algeria, *Résultats Statistiques de Dénombrement de la Population Effectué le 31 Octobre, 1954.*
Parlement, Avis et Rapports du Conseil Economique, 'Situation Economique et Sociale de l'Algérie', *Journal Officiel*, No. 10 (5 July 1955) (Delavignette Report).
Parlement, Conseil de le Republique, 'Projet de Loi', *Documents Parlementaries*, Annexe No. 133, Session 1941, Séance (21 March 1947) (UDMA Draft Statute).

MOVEMENT FOR THE TRIUMPH OF DEMOCRATIC LIBERTIES

NEWSPAPER

L'Algérie Libre

PAMPHLETS

Appel Aux Nations Unies (Paris, 1948).
Au Service du Peuple Algérien (Paris, 1947).
Deuxième Congrès National (n.p., n.d.).

SECONDARY MATERIALS

BOOKS

Alquier, Jean-Yves and others, *Ceux d'Algérie* (Paris: Librairie Plon, 1957).

Aron, Raymond, *La Tragedie Algérienne* (Paris: Librarie Plon, 1957).

Barberot, Roger, *Malaventure en Algérie* (Paris: Librarie Plon, 1957).

Bourdieu, Pierre, *Sociologie de l'Algérie* (Paris: Presses Universitaires de France, 1958).

Bousquet, G.-H., *L'Islam Maghrébin* (Alger: La Maison des Livres, 1941).

Brockelmann, Carl, *Histoire des Peuples et des Etats Islamiques* (Paris, Payot, 1949).

Bromberger, Merry and Serge, *Les 13 Complots du 13 Mai* (Paris: Librairie Arthème Fayard, 1958).

Bromberger, Serge, *Les Rebelles Algériens* (Paris: Librairie Plon, 1958).

Celier, Charles and others, *Industrialization de l'Afrique du Nord* (Paris: Librairie Armand Colin, 1952).

Chevallier, Jacques, *Nous, Algériens* (Paris: Calmann-Levy, 1958).

De Serigny, Alain, *La Revolution du 13 Mai* (Paris: Librairie Plon, 1958).

Despois, Jean, *L'Afrique du Nord* (Paris: Presses Universitaires de France, 1949).

Douxey, Jean, *S.O.S. Algérie* (Paris: Editions aux Carrefours du Monde, n.d.).

Earle, Edward Meade, ed., *Modern France* (Princeton: Princeton University Press, 1951).

Galibert, Leon, *L'Algérie* (Paris: Furne et Cie, 1844).

Gerin, Paul, *L'Algérie du 13 Mai* (Paris: Gallimard, 1958).

Guernier, Eugene Leonard, *La Berberie, L'Islam et la France* (Paris: Editions de l'Union Française, 1950).

Halpern, Manfred, *The French in Algeria*: 1944-7 (unpublished monograph, The School of Advanced International Studies, 1948).

Jeanson, Colette and Francis, *L'Algérie Hors la loi* (Paris: Editions du Seuil, 1955).

Juin, Maréchal, *Le Maghreb en Feu* (Paris: Librairie Plon, 1957).

Julien, Ch.-André, *L'Afrique du Nord en Marche* (Paris: Rene Julliard, 1952).

Histoire de l'Afrique du Nord (Paris: Payot, 1952).

Jung, Eugene, *Le Reveil de l'Islam et des Arabes* (Paris: chez l'Auteur, 1933).

Larnaude, Marcel, *Algérie* (Paris: Editions Berger-Levrault, 1950).

Lavie, Louis, *Le Drame Algérien* (Alger: Editions Baconnier, n.d.).

Luethy, Herbert, *France Against Herself* (New York: Frederick A. Praeger, Inc., 1955).

Mammeri, Mouloud, *Le Sommeil du Juste* (Paris: Librairie Plon, 1955).

Mitterand, François, *Présence Française et Abandon* (Paris: Librairie Plon, 1957).

Planchais, Jean, *Le Malaise de l'Armée* (Paris: Librairie Plon, 1958).

Sarrasin, Paul-Emile, *La Crise Algérienne* (Paris: Les Editions du Cerf, 1949).

Schoenbrun, David, *As France Goes* (New York: Harper and Bros., 1957).

Servan-Schreiber, Jean-Jacques, *Lieutenant in Algeria* (New York: Alfred A. Knopf, 1957).

Soustelle, Jacques, *Aimée et Souffrante Algérie* (Paris: Librairie Plon, 1956).

Soustelle, Jacques, *Le Drame Algérien et la Décadence Française* (Paris: Librarie Plon, 1957).

Stevens, Edmund, *North African Powder Keg* (New York: Coward-McCann, Inc., 1955).

Tillon, Germaine, *Algérie – The Realities* (London: Eyre and Spottiswoode, 1958).

PAMPHLETS

Études Sociales Nord-Africaines, *La Population Musulmane de l'Algérie*, Paris, No. 50 (January–February 1956).

France, Government-General of Algeria, *L'Algérie en 1830* (n.p., n.d.).

Levi-Provençal, E., *L'Emir Shakib Arslan* (1869-1946) (Paris, 1948).

ARTICLES

Chapelle, Dickey, Press Releases on Algeria, September 1957.

Cowan, L. Gray, 'The New Face of Algeria', *Political Science Quarterly*, Vol. 66, No. 3 (September 1951).

Duclos, Jacques, 'La Solution du Problème Algérien', *Cahiers du Communisme* (February 1957).

Lacheraf, Mostefa, 'Le Nationalisme Algérien: Sens d'une Revolution', *Les Temps Modernes*, Nos. 127-8 (September–October 1956).

Le Corre, Darius, 'De "l'Indépendance" de la Bretagne à "l'Indépendance" de l'Algérie', *Le Populaire de Paris* (10 October 1957).

Le Tourneau, Roger, Lecture series on Algeria, reprinted March 1957.

Oliver, Roland and Verrière, Louis, 'L'Economie Algérienne, Sa Structure – Son Evolution de 1950 à 1955,' *Études et Conjuncture*, No. 2 (February 1957).

'Le Parti Communist Algérien,' *Bulletin de l'Association d'Études et d'Informations Politiques Internationales*, No. 138 (16–31 October 1955).

Poirier, Lucien, 'Un Instrument de Guerre Révolutionnaire: Le, FLN,' *Revue Militaire d'Information* (December 1957).

Research and Information Commission of the International
    Student Conference, 'Reports on Higher Education in
    Algeria, Cuba, Cyprus, Hungary and Nicaragua', *RIC
    Yearbook, 1956-7* (n.d.).
'Les Ulemas Algériens Réformists,' *La Nouvelle Revue Française
    d'Outre Mer.*, Nos. 7-8 (July–August 1955).

Appendix

Nationalist Military Activity
November 1954–November 1958

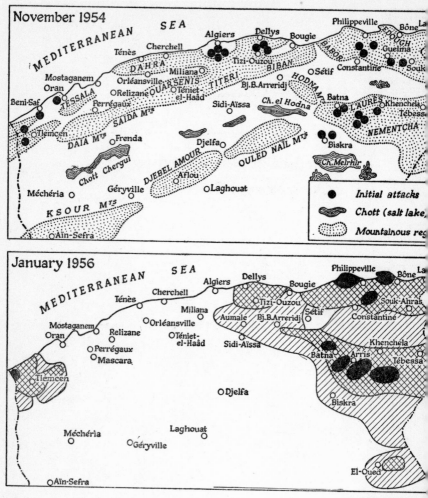

November 1954

MEDITERRANEAN SEA

Algiers Dellys Bougie Philippeville Bône La
Ténès Cherchell Tizi-Ouzou Guelma
DAHRA Miliana BIBAN Constantine Souk
Mostaganem Orléanville OUARSENIS TITERI Sétif
Oran Relizane Téniet HODNA Mᵗˢ
Beni-Saf TESSALA Perrégaux el-Haâd Bj.B.Arreridj Batna L'AURES Khenchela
Tlemcen SAIDA Mᵗˢ Sidi-Aïssa Ch. el Hodna Tébess
NEMENTCHA
DAIA Mᵗˢ Frenda Biskra
Djelfa OULED NAIL Mᵗˢ Ch.Melrhir
Chott Chergui DJEBEL AMOUR Aflou

Méchéria Géryville Laghouat

KSOUR Mᵗˢ

Aïn-Sefra

● Initial attacks

Chott (salt lake,

Mountainous reg

January 1956

MEDITERRANEAN SEA

Algiers Dellys Philippeville Bône La
Ténès Cherchell Bougie
Miliana Tizi-Ouzou Sétif Souk-Ahras
Orléansville Aumale Bj.B.Arreridj Constantine
Mostaganem Relizane Téniet- Khenchela
Oran Perrégaux el-Haâd Sidi-Aïssa Batna Arris
Mascara Tébessa
Tlemcen
Biskra
Djelfa

Méchéria Laghouat
Géryville

El-Oued

Aïn-Sefra

NATIONALI:
November 195

From January 1956 on, black sectors
indicate zones secured by nationalist
forces. In the cross-hatched areas
nationalist forces are able to introduce
a considerable degree of insecurity.

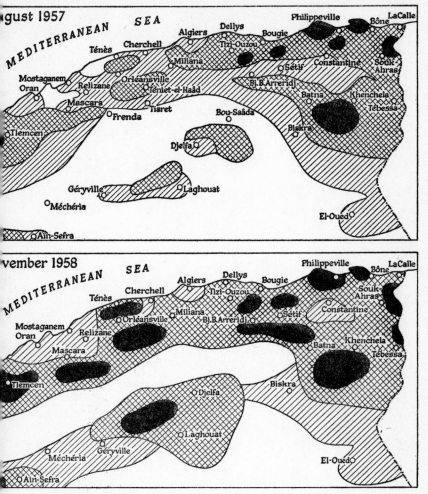

MILITARY ACTIVITY
November 1958

201

Index

Abane, Ramdane:
  and Council of Algerian Revolution,
    96-8, 100, 153
  and 'Operation Blue Bird', 151
  and the Kabyle *maquis*, 116
  CNRA conference, Cairo, 154
  his death, 104-5, 159
  opposes Ben Bella, 142
  personality, 105
  Soummam conference, 132
  strike of 1957, 152
Abbas, Ferhat, 66, 104
  and the Manifesto, 53-4
  appeals for calm, 1945, 58
  appeals to Muslim and French Alge-
    rian Youth, 62-3
  at the Conference of *Cadres*, 1954,
    74-5
  conflict with Messali, 57
  fails in election of 1951, 71
  forms UDMA, 62
  included in CCE, 100-1
  named as Prime Minister in Provi-
    sional Government, 102, 167
  placed under house arrest, 56
  proposes Algerian Constitution, 64
  publishes his views, 1931, 47
  replies to cease-fire offer, 183-4
  represents Federation, 1935, 47-8
  revolt of 1945, 58-9
  secret conversations with FLN, 118
  sponsors Muslim Congress, 1936, 49
  visits Cairo, 1956, 129
Accra, conference at, 161-2
Afro-Asian Peoples' Solidarity Conference, 148, 152-3, 160
Ait Ahmed, Hussein, 76, 94, 97, 99-100,
  102-3, 141
Aix-les-Bains, 129
Algeria:
  and de Gaulle, 181-4
  and foreign policy, 82
  and home rule, 125
  and Jacques Soustelle, 189
  and the *colons*, 22
  and the Manifesto, 54-5
  and the United Nations, 120, 185

  culture, 17, 172-3
  French prestige, 52
  its aims, 136-7
  leaders, 1956, 98
  Mahdia conference, 163
  Messali's influence, 42
  nationalism, 39
  original inhabitants, 17
  political parties – divergent views, 73
  population, 29
  rebellion extended, 1955, 120-1
  Referendum of 1958, 164-5
  relations with France, 50, 173-4
  revolution, 1954, 93
  riots, 145
  supported by Tunisia and Morocco,
    175-6, 183
Algerian Assembly, the, 26-7, 73, 121
*Algerian Front for the Defence and Respect
  of Liberty*, the, 73
Algerian-Moroccan border, 107
Algerian Nation, The, 85
Algerian National Congress, 82
Algerian Provisional Government, 174
  and insurrection in Algiers, 187
  and the United Nations, 171, 185-6
  CNRA announce foundation of pro-
    visional government, 167
  condemns elections, 170
  designates specific functions to mem-
    bers, 101
  meeting in Cairo, 169
  obtains limited recognition, 183
  seeks recognition, 144
  Tangier conference, 162
Algerian Resistance, the, FLN newspaper,
    148, 152-3
Algerian-Tunisian border, 29, 107, 116
Algiers, 19, 49, 67, 96, 105, 107
  battle of Algiers, 145-6, 149, 165-6
  CCE headquarters, 99
  Conference of *Cadres*, 74
  CRUA meetings, 95
  de Gaulle visits, 170
  insurrection January 1960, 187
  MTLD congress, 84
  population, 21, 29-30

Algiers prison, 153
Alsace-Lorraine, 8
Amara, Laksri, 97
Amis du Manifeste et de la Libérté (AML),
    56-7, 59-60, 62, 71
Arab Bureaux, the, 21
Arab League, 57, 59, 82, 113
Arab Nation, The, 45
Armée de Libération Nationale (ALN):
    attacks, 120
    initiated, 96
    key rôle in new régime, 175
    leaders captured, 99
    Morice Line, the, 152
    problems, 116
    referendum, 165-7
    reorganized, 132-3
    represented by FLN in negotiations,
        142
    strategy, 110-11
    strength of, 123, 125
    structure, 107-10
    supported by Algerian people, 130
Arms and ammunition, shortage of,
    116-17
Arslan, Chekib, 42, 45
Atlantic Charter, the, 11, 59
Atlantic Pact, the, 79
Aurès, the, 76, 95-6, 104, 116, 147
Australia, 185

Baghdad, 108
Bangdung Conference, the, 119-20, 140
Barbarossa, Horuk and Khair-ed-Din,
    18
Barbary pirates, 18
Beeley, Mr., British Foreign office, 161
Begarra, M., 142
Belgium, 41
Bellounis, 'General', 150
Ben Aouda, 97
Ben Badis, Sheik Abdelhamid, 44-5, 47,
    84
Ben Bella, Ahmed, 76, 94, 97, 99-104,
    141-2, 147, 167, 185
Ben Boulaid, Mostefa, 94-5, 97, 104,
    116-17
Ben Boulaid, Omar, 132
Bendjelloul, Dr., 48-9, 54, 62, 118
Beni-Oui-Oui (Yes-men), 72, 121
Benkhedda, Benyoussef, 82-4, 96-9, 102,
    186
Ben M'Hidi, Mohamed Larbi, 94-5,
    97-9, 104-5, 126, 132, 153
Ben Tobbal, Lakhdar, 96-7, 100-1, 132
Ben Yahia, Mohamed, 97
Ben Youssef, Salah, 117, 120
Berbers, the, 78-9, 105, 116, 141
Bidault, M., 184

Bitat, Rabat, 94-5, 97, 100, 102, 153
Bizerte, 161, 176-7
Blachette, Georges, 12
Blida, 21
Bloc of Algerian Elected Muslims, 39
Blum, Premier Léon, 11, 24
Blum-Violette Proposal, the, 11, 24-5,
    42, 48, 64
Bône, 21, 30
Borgeaud, Senator Henri, 12
Bouda, 84
Boudiaf, Mohamed, 94-5, 98-100, 102-3,
    141
Boumediene, 97
Boumandjel, Ahmed, 72, 153, 163
Bourgès-Manoury, Government of, 154-
    5, 157
Bourguiba, President Habib, 117, 147,
    157, 159-61, 177, 183
Boussouf, Abdelhafid, 96-7, 100-1, 126
Bouzareah, 66
Brazzaville, 58
Brioni, meeting at, 143
Bugeaud, General, 6, 21

Cairo, 97, 99, 101, 103, 119, 129, 140,
    142, 147, 153-6, 160, 167-9
Casbah, the, Algiers, 146
Catroux, General, 13, 55-6, 127-8
Census:
    of 1936, 9
    of 1948, 29
Charles X, King, 6
Charles Martel, King, 18
Chataigneau, Yves, Governor-General,
    1944, 57-9, 70-1
Cherif, Mahmoud, 97, 100-1, 147
Chevallier, Jacques, Mayor of Algiers,
    72
Chihani, Bachir, 96, 116
China, revolution in, comparison, 125
Chinese People's Army, 171-2
Clemenceau, Premier George, 10, 24,
    39
Cold War, the, 70
Collo, 120
Commin, M. Pierre, 143-4
Comité de Co-ordination et Execution (CCE),
    98-100, 145, 147, 153-4, 156, 161,
    163
*Comité Révolutionnaire Pour L'Unité et
    L'Action* (CRUA), 94-6, 112, 141-2
Communism, 47, 49, 118
    Afro-Asian Peoples' Solidarity Con-
        ference, 160
    agents watched, 46
    alleged Communist-rebel collusion,
        122
    and Messali, 40

Communism—*cont.*
  and the ALN, 166
  and the battle of Algiers, 146
  and the ENA, 40-3
  and the unions, 130
  banned, 121
  establishment and progress, 64-7
  internal Communism, 176-7
  opinions of UDMA, 73-4
  party publishes *El Ouma*, 41
Confédération Générale du Travail, 130
Conference of *Cadres*, 1954, 74
Conseil National de le Révolution Algérienne
  (CNRA), 96-100, 142, 167
Constantine, 21-2, 29-30, 45, 48, 58,
  67, 76, 95-6, 116-17, 120-1, 132,
  168
Coty, President, 150
Cuba, 181

Dahlab, Saad, 96, 98-9
Daniel, Jean, 13
Debré, Premier Michel, 184
Delavignette, Robert:
  Report of 1955, 33-5
Deys of Algiers, 19, 130
Dhiles, Colonel Slimane, 97, 154
Didouche, Mourad, 94-5
Dien Bien Phu, 111, 129
Duval, French Consul, 6

East Germany, 108
Ecuador, 185
Education, 19, 27, 35-6, 46
Egypt, 140
Eisenhower, General, 183
El Azhar University, Cairo, 46
Elections, 62, 70-2
El Fassi, Allal, 120
El Haddad, Sheikh, 125
El Moudjahid, official FLN newspaper,
  108, 131, 159
El Ouma, 41
Equality, weekly journal of the AML,
  57-8
Erlon, General Drouet d', 7-8
Esterhazy, General, 8
Ethiopia, Italian invasion of, 42
Etoile Nord Africaine (ENA), 40-2, 49
European Payments Union, 159
Express, L', 13
External delegation, 142, 144-5, 147

Fajon, Etienne, 65
Federation of Elected Muslims, the, 47, 62
Ferroukhi, 84

Ferry, Jules, 10, 12
Financial delegations, 10, 22-3, 25
Foreign Legion, 140
France, 14-16, 30-1, 35, 54, 59, 68, 70,
  72-3, 77, 104, 113-15, 117, 119,
  127, 136-7, 146, 148-9, 173, 176,
  186, 190
France, defeat of, 1940, 52
France, Government of, 24, 41-2, 48,
  55-6, 67, 126-9, 135, 137, 143,
  149-51, 155-8, 160-1, 165, 167-8,
  177, 184-5, 189
France Observateur, 123, 129
Francis, Ahmed, 97, 102, 163
Franco-Muslim Algerian Rally, the, 40
Free Algeria, organ of the MTLD, 82-4
Freedom Fighter, the, 153
French Administration, 6-10, 21-7, 39,
  46-7, 54, 72, 74, 120-1, 135
French Army, the, 27, 40, 119, 121-3,
  128, 132, 136, 146, 150, 154, 162,
  164-70, 174
French Economic Council, 33
French Resistance, the, 110
French Union Assembly, the, 4
Front de Libération Nationale (FLN):
  and de Gaulle, 190
  and the 'Melouza massacre', 150
  and the referendum, 167
  and the United Nations, 126, 143-4,
    148-9
  battle of Algiers, 145-7, 149
  Communist influence, 166
  demands recognition, 137-8
  extends propaganda activities, 152-3,
    155
  extends rebellion, August 1955, 121-3
  external delegation, 129, 143
  FLN-French negotiations, 148, 154,
    156, 158, 168, 182, 187
  formed, 96
  founds UGTA, 129-30
  its political affiliations, 117-19
  its principles, 123-8, 149
  leadership, 99
  Muslim support, 151
  obtains support, 112-15
  participates in Accra conference,
    162-3
  participates in Afro-Asian Peoples'
    Solidarity Conference, 160
  reactions to the Mollet visit, 129
  relations with Tunisia and Morocco,
    117, 119, 125
  reorganizes leadership, 153
  Soummam conference, 98, 133-4,
    138-9, 141-2
  strike of 1957, 152
  structure, 106
  Tangier meeting, 101

Gaillard Government, the, 159, 161
Garibaldi, Giuseppe, 8
Gaulle, General Charles de, 167, 174, 185-6
and insurrection in Algiers, 187-9
and the Manifesto, 55
and the Muslims, 25, 164
becomes Premier, 164
dismisses General Massu, 188
during World War II, 52
his responsibilities in the Algerian War, 190
influences changes, 57
instructs French delegation to United Nations, 171
negotiates with Algerian rebels, 168-70, 182-3
receives power to rule by decree for one year, 189
visits overseas territories, 164, 170
Geneva, 42, 129
Glorious Star, the, 41
Goeau-Brissonnière, M., 155-6
Gorse, M., 142
Great Britain, 140, 161, 185
Guelma, 120

Haussonvillers, 76
Heliopolis, Congress of, 57
Hilalian invasion, 18
Hitler, Adolf, 65
Honduras, 185
Hornu, Belgium, 84

Ibrahimi, Sheik, 45, 56, 59, 83
Income distribution, 33-5
Independent Muslim Group for the Defence of Algerian Federalism, 67
Indo-China, war in, 5, 70, 111, 150, 165, 166
Industry, 36
International Confederation of Free Trade Unions, 155
International Monetary Fund, 159
Istiqlal, Moroccan party, 101, 120, 162
Italy, 132, 168

Kabyles, the, 8, 20, 76, 102, 105, 108, 116, 132, 151, 154
Kabylia, 20, 22, 78, 95, 103, 116
Kader, Emir Abd El, 19-20, 39
Khaled, Emir, grandson of Abd El Kader, 39-40, 44
Khider, Mohamed, 43, 66-7, 76, 94, 98-100, 102, 141, 143
Kiouane, Abderrahmane, 82-4
Krim, Belkacem, 94-5, 98, 100-3, 116, 132, 153,167

Labour force, distribution of, 32-3
Lacoste, Robert, Governor-General, 1956, 70, 128, 165
Lahouel, Hussein, 43, 66, 82-4
Lamine-Debaghine, Dr. Mohamed, 66-7, 78-9, 97-8, 100-1, 142, 147, 153, 155, 160, 167, 186
Lamine-Gueye law of 1946, 25
Lamine-Khan, 102
Lamouri, 98
Laos, 185
Latin America, 140-1, 162
Laval, Pierre, 11
Lavie, Louis, 14
League of Nations, 41
Le Monde, 127
Leonard, M., Governor-General, 71
Liberty, weekly organ of the Algerian Communist Party, 65
Libya, 132, 140-1, 147
London, 52, 140
Louanchi, 84
Louis Philippe, King, 6

Maghreb Consultative Assembly, 162, 176
Mahdia, conference at, 161, 163-4
Mahsas, Ahmed, 98
Manifesto of the Algerian People, 53-6, 60, 62, 103
Mao Tse-tung, 110
Mascara, 21
Maspétiol, M., 34
Massu, General Jacques, 146, 152, 165, 187-8
Mecca, 77
Medea, 21
Mehri, Abdelhamid, 97-8, 100-2
Mellah, Ali, 98, 132
Melouza, 149-50
Mendès-France, Pierre, Premier, 116
Merbah, Moulay, 84-5
Messali Ahmed Ben Hadj, 47, 57, 59, 74, 95, 117, 123, 132, 135, 139, 150
and elections of 1946, 66-7
and MTLD, 77, 82-7, 103
and the PPA, 43-4, 64-5
associations with Communist Party, 41, 66
attempted domination of national movement, 102
creates ENA, 40-1
disagrees with Lamine, 79
early life, 40
excludes leaders from MTLD, 84-6
founds MTLD, 66
house arrest in France, 76-7
house arrest in Reibell, 52
imprisoned, 42

Messali Ahmed Ben Hadj—*cont.*
  life reviewed in *Free Algeria*, 84
  policies opposed, 81
  proposes round-table conference, 129
  rejects suggested reforms, 56
  returns to Bouzareah, 66
  sent to Brazzaville, 58
  sponsors Muslim Congress, Algiers, 49
Mezerna, Ahmed, 43, 66-7, 77, 84-5
Mezhoudi, Brahim, 98
Michelet Street, Algiers, bombs exploded, 146
Mitterand, Senator, 184
Mohammed V, King, 157, 159, 183
Mollet, Guy, Prime Minister, 127-9, 142-5, 156, 169
Monnerot, Jules, 91
Morice Line, the, 152
Morocco, 5, 17, 70, 74, 78, 84, 94, 101, 108, 119, 125, 129, 131, 135, 139, 144-5, 148, 156-8, 162-3, 175-7
Moroccan Army of Liberation, 126
Moscow, 140
Mostefai, UDMA leader, 68
Mouvement National Algérien (MNA), 117-18, 122-3, 129, 150
Mouvement pour la Triomphe des Libertés Démocratiques (MTLD), 66-8, 70-1, 73-4, 76-87, 95-7, 103, 116, 150
Municipal Stadium of Algiers, 42
Murphy, Mr., U.S. State Department, 161
Muslim Congress, Algiers, 49
Muslim Congress, Geneva, 42
Muslim Economic and Social Affairs, Commission for the Study of, 54

Nador, Spanish Morocco, 126
Naegelen, Marcel-Edmond, Governor-General, 1948, 70-1
Napoleon III, 6-8, 20, 22
Nasser, Gamal Abdel, 143
Nasser, 96, 116
National Union of North African Muslims, 41
Native Code, the, 21, 23
NATO, 79, 140, 174, 177
Naturalization law of 1889, 31
Nehru, Jawaharlal, 143
Neo-Destour, Tunisian party, 101, 117, 120, 162
New York, 127
Nicaragua, 185
Niort, France, 84-5
Nouaroua, 96, 132

Oil supplies from the Sahara, 149
Okbi, Sheik El, 45

Oran, 29-30, 76, 95-6, 103-4, 126, 147
Ordinances, 20, 24-5, 56
Organization Speciale (OS), 76, 95, 103
Orléansville, earthquake of 1954, 94
Ouamrane, Amar, 96, 100, 101, 116, 123-4, 126, 132, 147, 151
Oued-Zem, Morocco, 120
Oujda, 126
Ouseddik, Omar, 102, 186

Paraguay, 185
Paris, 7, 9-10, 15, 40, 42, 49, 99, 141, 153, 161, 168, 174, 184, 187
Parlement Algérien, Le, 43
Parti du Peuple Algérien, the (PPA), 43-4, 49, 50, 56-7, 59, 64-6, 76
Peking, visited by Provisional Algerian Government, 171-2
Pétain, Marshal Henri Philippe, 11
Pétain régime, the, 43
Philippeville, 120
Poitiers, 18
Popular Algerian Union, the, 49
Population structure, 31-2

Rabat, 101, 144, 157, 163, 167, 169
Radio Cairo, 153
Radio Free Algeria, 152
Radio Tunis, 153
Referendum of 1958, 164-7
'Régime of Decrees', 26
Regnier Decree, the, 42, 49
Regnier, M., French Minister of the Interior, 48
Reibell, South Algeria, 52, 56
Religious influences, 18-19, 25, 27, 104, 135, 174
Rome, meetings at, 143

Sahara, the, 29, 36, 132, 149, 170, 173, 175, 182
Sakiet Sidi Youssef, 160-1, 177
San Francisco Conference, 59
Santé Prison, Paris, 144
Saudi Arabia, Government of, 119
Scandinavia, 140
School of Oriental Languages, 40
Senatus Consulte of 1863, 20, 24
Sétif, 47, 58, 62, 71
Sidi-Ali-Bounab, 76
Sidi Ferruch, 6
Sinn Fein movement, 110
Socialist Party of France, 67
Soummam Valley, conference at, 97-8, 107-8, 131-3, 137, 139, 141-2, 145, 154

Soustelle, Jacques, Governor-General, 1955, 121, 151, 168, 184, 189
Soviet Union, 77
Spain, 140-1
Stambouli, Mustafa, 102
Statute for Algeria, 1947, 25-7, 59, 68, 70-87
Suddeutsche Zeitung, 188
Suez crisis, the, 5, 147-8, 165, 177
Suidani, 96
Superior Council of Algeria, 10
Switzerland, 42, 95, 168
Syria, 23

Tangier, conferences at, 101, 161-3
Tax collection system, FLN, 145
Tebessi, Sheik Larbi, 129
Tewfik-El-Madani, 97-8, 102, 118, 129, 186
Thaalbi, Tayeb, 98
Thorez, Maurice, 64
Tillon, M., French Minister for Air, 58
Tito, Marshal, 143
Tlemcem, 21, 23, 40, 42, 126
Touggourt, 170
Tunis, 101, 104, 144, 147, 153, 155-6, 161, 163, 167, 169
Tunisia, 5, 17, 70, 74, 78, 84, 94, 99, 101, 108, 117, 119, 125, 131, 135, 139, 144-5, 147-8, 151-2, 156-8, 160, 162-3, 175-6
Turkish rule, 18

Ulema, *Society of Reformist*, 44-7, 49-50, 56, 66, 73-4, 79-80, 83, 97, 118, 129
Union Démocratique du Manifeste Algérien (UDMA), 62-3, 66-8, 71-5, 79-80, 82, 97, 100, 102, 118, 153, 163

Union Générale des Commercants Algériens (UGCA), 130
Union Générale des Etudiants Musulmans Algériens (UGEMA), 130
Union Générale des Travailleurs Algériens (UGTA), 129
United Nations, 113, 119-20, 126-7, 143, 148-50, 152, 155-6, 158-9, 170-1, 174, 181, 186
United States of America, 13, 35, 77, 140-1, 159, 161, 171, 176-7, 185-6
University of Algiers, 35
University of Bordeaux, 40

Vichy Government, 43, 52
Victoria, Queen, 8
Viet Minh, 166
Vietnam, 150
Villeurbanne Congress, 1935, 64
Vision of the Future, The, 45

Warnier law of 1873, 21
Washington, 121, 140
World War I, 9-10, 39-40
World War II, 11, 23, 52-60, 94, 103, 110

Yazid, M'Hammed, 84, 97-8, 102, 119, 143, 155, 185
Young Algerian, The, 47
Young Algerian Party, the, 23
Yugoslav guerrilla warfare, 110

Zirout, Youssef, 96-8, 132
Zitouna University, Algiers, 44, 46

Printed in Great Britain by
The Camelot Press Ltd., London and Southampton